LEGAL LIMITS OF AUTHORITY

OVER THE PUPIL

by

Edward C. Bolmeier

Professor Emeritus of Education
Duke University
Durham, North Carolina

THE MICHIE COMPANY

Law Publishers

CHARLOTTESVILLE, VIRGINIA

Dedication

To my wife,
Hazel, cheerful
companion, counsellor,
critic.

Contents

Chapter 1 INTRODUCTION

Chapter 2 COMPULSORY AND PROHIBITORY
SCHOOL ATTENDANCE

Chapter 3 AUTHORITY OVER CURRICULAR
ACTIVITIES

Chapter 1

INTRODUCTION

§ 1.1. Judicial task to determine authority.

Allocation of authority over the pupil has been a matter of dispute and litigation ever since the beginning of public education in America. The courts have been called upon repeatedly to settle issues concerning "parental versus state authority over the pupil."

The judicial task of delimiting family and school authority over the pupil is a difficult one. The pupil, as a subject of the state, is entitled to the rights and freedoms thereof, and at the same time he is subject to those regulations of the state which are designed for the health, safety, progress and general welfare of the populace. But the pupil is also a member of the family, and, in this capacity, is subject to the care and control of parents.

When clashes between the family and the school arise over matters concerning the pupil's welfare, the courts must take into consideration the natural rights as well

1

as the civil rights of pupils and their parents. *Natural rights* are considered to be "inalienable," "fundamental" and "inherent"; they are rights necessary to personal liberty, security and the pursuit of happiness. *Civil rights*, on the other hand, are those rights which pertain to an individual by virtue of his citizenship or residence in a community or state. Whereas natural rights are considered to exist outside of law and independent of government, civil rights exist under law guaranteed by federal and state constitutions. Civil rights include personal freedoms such as religious liberty, freedom of speech, security against unreasonable search and seizure, the guaranty against self-incrimination, the right to trial by jury, and the right to equal protection of the laws. Both natural rights and civil rights, such as those enumerated, are frequently brought into focus when pupils and their parents challenge, in the courts, unfavorable actions of school officials. Then on the basis of humanity and law the courts make the final decisions.

§ 1.2. Scope of issues to be reported.

Most of the litigation pertinent to "parental (family) versus state (school) authority over the pupil (student)" falls into three main categories. The first has to do with *compulsory and prohibitory school attendance*. Here questions such as the following arise: May the state require *public* school attendance against the parents' wishes? What are legal alternatives to *public* school attendance? May a child be exempted from attending any school for certain reasons? May school officials enforce vaccination requirements as a condition for school attendance? Does dual enrolment violate compulsory school attendance laws? May unwed mothers be denied school attendance?

A second area of litigation relates to *authority* over *curriculum activities* of the school. Typical questions in this area frequently brought before the courts are: May the pupil be compelled to pursue a required course? May the state prohibit the teaching of a foreign language? May the state prohibit the teaching of evolution? May a pupil be required to pledge allegiance to and salute the American flag? May a pupil be required to participate in religious exercises? May a married student be barred from non-classroom activities?

The third, and most frequently litigated area, involves *control over student behavior*. The more controversial issues in this area, contested in the courts in recent years, are indicated by the following questions: May school officials regulate attire and personal appearance of the student? May a student be prohibited from displaying insignia as a form of protest? May school authorities restrict the student's freedom of speech and press? May school personnel search and permit others to search student lockers? Do school personnel have authority and responsibility over pupil behavior away from or after school? May school officials prohibit student affiliation with secret societies?

§ 1.3. Selection and treatment of court cases.

Just brief reference to every court case dealing with all aspects of compulsory school attendance, curriculum activities, and control over student behavior would constitute an undertaking beyond and aside that designed for this publication. Therefore only a reasonable sampling of those cases which appear to be most pertinent to the research project, as indicated by the title, have been selected for analysis and report.

Special effort was made to identify those cases in which the relative authority of the parents and the state over the pupil was the dominant issue. Excerpts were extracted and quoted from the case reports which indicated judicial opinions as to relative authority.

Although many of the litigated issues involving "parental versus state authority over the pupil" culminated in lower court decisions, nearly all the cases treated herein were those decided by courts of record (federal and higher state courts). All United States Supreme Court cases which have had a direct bearing on the research project have been included. Since the Civil Rights Act of 1964, many of the court cases involving certain student rights have been carried to and disposed of in the federal district court and federal courts of appeals; a sampling of those which are most germane to the investigation were selected for treatment.

In order to make the report as up-to-date as possible the most recent applicable court cases have been sought and included. Nevertheless, many of the earlier cases which established rather firm legal principles or trends are reported. It is realized by the writer that during the interim between completion of the manuscript and its actual publication some very significant court decisions pertaining to the subject will have been rendered. That, however, is a reason why research is never terminal.

Those cases which have been selected for inclusion in this research project are reported as succinctly as possible. The pertinent facts leading up to the case are reported first. Then the decision of the court is indicated. Whenever the courts make specific statements pertaining to the relative limits of parental or state authority over the pupil, excerpts from the courts' dicta are quoted verbatim. No attempt is made to *evaluate* constitutional and statutory provisions, school board policies, or court decisions. The main purpose of the concluding chapter is to indicate guiding legal principles, emanating from court decisions referred to in the main chapters.

§ 1.4. Variation in terminology.

It may be noted that certain words or terms in this report are used interchangeably. For example, in referring to "parental authority" over the pupil, the term "family authority" could be substituted. The former conveys the authority a parent has over his minor offspring as originally determined by common law; the latter denotes, in addition, the authority a minor possesses over himself. This is particularly significant now since recent court decisions have indicated applicability of the Fourteenth Amendment and Bill of Rights to all, regardless of age or status (*In re Gault*, 387 U.S. 1, 13, 1967).

Usually when a pupil who is a minor is involved in litigation he is joined by a parent appointed as guardian *ad litem* to prosecute or defend the suit on behalf of the pupil incapacitated by infancy. Hence "family authority" is somewhat broader in meaning than "parental authority" since it includes both pupil and parents.

Also, since the school district is merely a territorial subdivision of the state for school purposes, the terms "state" and "school" may, in certain situations, be used synonymously. Whether the legality of a school action stems from a state law or a school board regulation is of no consequence as far as deprivation of parental authority over the pupil is concerned. Moreover, even though school administrators and teachers are not state officers, their actions toward pupils, if supported or directed by school boards, are of as much concern to parents as if they were direct actions of state officials.

A writer may be uncertain sometimes as to when the term "pupil" or "student" should be used in referring to a youth attending a secondary school. One who attends an elementary school is usually referred to as a pupil, whereas one enrolled in an institution of higher learning is referred to as a "student." Those attending a high school, however, may be called either. There is no consistency in the educational literature with respect to usage of the two terms. Even the courts frequently use both terms in referring to a party in a particular case. Therefore interchangeability of the terms in this publication is in line with common practice.

Chapter 2

COMPULSORY AND PROHIBITORY
SCHOOL ATTENDANCE

§ 2.1. Evolving concepts of authority over attendance.

Exclusive parental authority. — It has always been accepted that the welfare of the child and that of society in general required an educational opportunity. Nevertheless in the early stages of our educational development, the state did not compel parents to enter their children in school, even though the opportunity was available. At common law it was the duty of parents to give their children an education suitable to their status in life. Unfortunately, however, the common law stopped short of guaranteeing that such duty be performed. Customs had been established that the state should provide the means for the child's education, but the state left it to the parents and guardians to deter-

7

mine the extent to which the education would be made available to the children under their charge.

Early court cases indicated the early concept of parental discretion in determining the extent of the child's education. For example, in an Illinois case (*Rulison* v. *Post*, 79 Ill. 567, 1876), a court declared in 1896 that:

> Parents and guardians are under the responsibility of preparing children intrusted to their care and nurture, for the discharge of their duties in after life. Law-givers in all free countries, and, with few exceptions, in despotic governments, have deemed it wise to leave the education and nurture of the children of the State to the direction of the parent or guardian. This is, and has ever been, the spirit of our free institutions. The State has provided the means, and brought them within the reach of all, to acquire the benefits of a common school education, but leaves it to the parents and guardians to determine the extent to which they will render it available to the children under their charge. (*Id.* at 573)

Just one year later, in another Illinois case (*Trustees of Schools* v. *People*, 87 Ill. 303, 1877), the Supreme Court of Illinois gave judicial credence to this early concept by stating:

> ... the policy of our law has ever been to recognize the right of the parent to determine to what extent the child shall be educated, ... presuming that the natural affections and superior opportunities of knowing the physical and mental capabilities and future prospects of his child, will insure the adoption of that course which will most effectually promote the child's welfare. (*Id.* at 308)

Public reaction. — Gradually the public recognized that the early common law which authorized absolute parental control over the child's education sometimes resulted in deprivation of the child's welfare as well as that of society. The courts especially were critical of practice which permitted parents to keep their children out of school if they so desired. Excerpts of an early Georgia case (*Board of Education* v. *Purse*, 101 Ga. 422, 28 S.E. 896, 1897) are indicative:

> While the common law recognizes this as a duty of great importance, there was no remedy provided for the child in case this duty was not discharged by the parent. The child, at the will of the parent, could be allowed to grow up in ignorance, and become a more than useless member of society, and for this great wrong, brought about by the neglect of his parents, the common law provided no remedy. Not only no remedy was given to the child, but no punishment was inflicted upon the parent. (*Id.* at 899)

> ... Neither the school authorities nor any court could compel the child for its own interest to enter the school, or remain in it, without the parent's consent, and, where that consent is not given on the terms rightly prescribed by the school board, it is the same as withheld, or not given at all. (*Id.* at 901)

In order to remove the potential cruelties of the early common law which denied the state any control over the child's education against his parents' wishes, lawmakers considered the constitutionality of legislation which would give the state such power.

Judicial sanction of state authority. — Legislatures were quickly supported by the courts to enact compulsory school attendance laws by virtue of (1) *police power* which is acknowledged as authority residing in every sovereignty to pass laws judged to be good and for the welfare of the state and residents; and (2) *power of parens patriae* which is considered to be the inherent power and authority of a lawmaking body to provide protection for legally incapable persons such as minors.

Bolstered by judicial sanction to exercise *police power* and *power of parens patriae* in enacting and implementing compulsory school attendance laws, all fifty states have enacted such legislation. However, shortly after the *Brown* decision of 1954, South Carolina (in 1955), Mississippi (in 1956) and Virginia (in 1959) repealed their compulsory school attendance statutes enacted by earlier legislatures.

In many instances the constitutionality of the compulsory school attendance laws was challenged in the courts, with the allegation that they violated the natural rights of parents to control the welfare of their children. Despite the hesitancy of some courts to break away from the early common law precedents, the Indiana Supreme Court rendered a decision in 1901 which settled the issue firmly and permanently by ruling that the power of the state was sufficient to justify compulsory school attendance laws.

In this early case (*State* v. *Bailey*, 157 Ind. 324, 61 N.E. 730, 1901) a parent was charged with having neglected and refused to send his child to school, thereby violating the provisions of the state's compulsory school attendance law. The parent alleged that the law was unconstitutional because "it invades the natural right of a man to govern and control his own children." The court, however, ruled in favor of the state, holding that the law did not conflict with the constitutional guarantee of individual rights. In refuting the claims of the parent, the court stated:

> The natural rights of a parent to the custody and control of his infant child are subordinate to the power of the state, and may be restricted and regulated by municipal laws. One of the most important natural duties of the parent is his obligation to educate his child, and this duty he owes not to the child only, but to the commonwealth. If he neglects to perform it or willingly refuses to do so, he may be coerced by law to execute such civil obligations. The welfare of the child and the best interests of society require that the state shall exert its sovereign authority to secure to the child the opportunity to acquire an education. Statutes making it compulsory upon the parent, guardian, or other person having the custody and control of children to send them to public or private schools for longer or shorter periods during certain years of the life of such children have not only been upheld as strictly within the constitutional power of the legislature, but have generally been regarded necessary to carry out the express purposes of the constitution itself. (*Id.* at 731-32)

§ 2.2. Alternatives to public school attendance.

Attendance at nonpublic schools. — After the main issue of compulsory school attendance had been resolved, the question arose as to whether or not the attendance requirement could be met by attending a *nonpublic* school. Even after the public school system had been generally accepted, there were those who wished for their children to attend a private — particularly parochial — school. However, some legislators and other citizens who feared that divisiveness in the American school system would jeopardize its effectiveness, sought to compel *public* school attendance. As legislation to that effect was enacted its constitutionality was vigorously challenged on the grounds that it violated natural and inalienable rights of parents to exercise control over their children.

Undoubtedly the most important and conclusive decision on the issue which legally sanctioned the perpetuity of *nonpublic* schools was that handed down by the United States Supreme Court in the Oregon compulsory public school attendance case (*Pierce* v. *Society of Sisters of Holy Names*, 268 U.S. 510, 45 S. Ct. 571, 1925). The litigation in this case emanated from an Oregon law enacted in 1922, which required children between the ages of eight and sixteen to attend *public* schools. The obvious purpose of the law was to eliminate *private* elementary and middle schools. The Supreme Court referred to the provisions of the Fourteenth Amendment as nullifying legislation designed to "deprive any person of life, liberty, or property without due process of law."

The notable decision of the Oregon case demonstrates the constitutional protection of parents' right to send their children to schools of their own choice. The classic declaration of the Court is forceful and has been generally unchallenged:

> ... we think it entirely plain that the Act of 1922 unreasonably interferes with the liberty of parents and guardians to direct the upbringing and education of children under their control. .... The fundamental theory of liberty upon which all governments in this Union repose excludes any general power of the state to standardize its children by forcing them to accept instruction from public teachers only. The child is not the mere creature of the state; those who nurture him and direct his destiny have the right, coupled with the high duty, to recognize and prepare him for additional obligations. (*Id.* at 573)

Home instruction. — Some parents have sought to satisfy compulsory school attendance requirements by providing *home instruction* rather than by attending either public or nonpublic schools. The legality of the practice cannot be determined simply or conclusively; the phrasing of the applicable statutes, the interpretations of the courts placed upon them, as well as numerous other factors, are determinants. Nevertheless, under certain conditions, home instruction has been, and still is, legally sanctioned as satisfying compulsory school attendance requirements.

Even though some states approve home instruction in lieu of public or private school instructions as meeting the compulsory school attendance laws, they limit that approval by requiring that the home instruction meet specified standards. An illustrative case (*Rice* v. *Commonwealth*, 188 Va. 224, 49 S.E.2d 342, 1948) came before the Supreme Court of Virginia in 1948. Here the state law provided that in the absence of satisfactory public or private school attendance, parents might comply with the law by having their children taught by a tutor or teacher whose qualifications meet those prescribed by the State Board of Education and approved by the division superintendent of schools.

The parents involved in this case were deeply religious, and rather than sending their children to public schools "where they may be subjected to unwholesome influences," they attempted to provide the instruction themselves. They disregarded the fact that their professional qualifications did not meet those prescribed by the State Board, and approved by the division superintendent of schools. Consequently they were charged with a violation of the compulsory school attendance law and convicted accordingly.

In support of its ruling the court stated that:

> ... in order to impart an education to a child, it is self-evident that the instructor must himself have adequate learning and training in the art of teaching. Obviously, an illiterate parent cannot properly educate his child, nor can he, by attempting to do so, avoid his obligation to send it to school. No amount of religious fervor he may entertain in opposition to adequate instruction should be allowed to work a lifelong injury to his child. Nor should he for this religious reason, be suffered to inflict another illiterate citizen on his community or his state.... (*Id.* at 348)

Another defense of the parents was that the jury, not the school authorities, should determine whether the parents were adequately qualified to instruct their children. In disagreeing with this contention, and supporting state requirements that the designated public officials should make the decision, the court added that the local division superintendents ". . . are themselves required to be well-informed and well-versed in the field of education. They are undoubtedly much better equipped to pass upon a parent's qualification as a teacher than the ordinary laymen who comprise nearly all juries. In order to appraise intelligently such qualifications, it is necessary to carry on an investigation into the experience, character, and ability of the parent as a teacher. This inquiry obviously cannot be conducted by a jury, the members of which are themselves not required to be qualified to teach or learned in the profession." (*Id.* at 349)

Stringency of requirements. — Compulsory school attendance laws of some states are rather stringent and do not allow alternatives for attendance at a public or private school taught by a competent instructor. For example, the law of Kansas does not permit mere equivalency. There the statute must be adhered to strictly; exemption from school attendance is only on the basis of physical or mental incapacity.

A case in point (*State* v. *Garber* (Kan.), 419 P.2d 896, 1966), is where a parent (member of Old Order Mennonite Church) of a 15-year-old daughter, was found guilty of violating the compulsory school attendance law, even though the child was given *home* instruction in lieu of *school* instruction.

The court ruled that: "Even if system of education consisting essentially of home instruction was considered as instruction equivalent to that given in public, private, denominational or parochial school, as required by compulsory school attendance law, such would not constitute excuse for nonattendance at latter, in view of fact that Legislature made no provision for such equivalent instruction as basis for exemption." (*Id.* at 896)

The court considered further whether or not the statute requiring attendance at a school violated religious liberty guaranteed by the Federal Constitution. Commenting on this point the court declared:

> ... we are unable to perceive from the record before us how religious freedom is abridged in this case. There is no infringement upon the right to worship or to believe insofar as either defendant or his daughter is concerned. Their freedoms to worship and believe remain absolute and are not affected by our compulsory school attendance law. Defendant may instruct his daughter in religious beliefs as he desires. ... No matter how sincere he may be the individual cannot be permitted upon religious grounds to be the judge of his duty to obey laws enacted in the public interest. We think the particular law at issue here is valid as applied to defendant and his daughter and does not infringe upon constitutionally guaranteed religious freedom. (*Id.* at 902)

Permissible home instruction. — Usually courts tend to support reasonable "home school" standards which are clearly stipulated in the compulsory school attendance laws. Unfortunately the laws are not always clear and specific. In such instances the courts must determine what the legislative intent was. A case in point was decided by the Criminal Court of Appeals of Oklahoma in 1922 (*Wright* v. *State*, 21 Okla. 430, 209 P. 179, 1922).

Here a parent had been convicted before a lower court for violating the state's compulsory school attendance law, in that he failed to send his daughter to a "public or private school, unless other means of education are provided."

Testimony revealed that both the mother and father of the child were well qualified and experienced for the instruction of children. Moreover, there was evidence that the child involved showed considerable proficiency in the various school subjects.

The state argued, however, that the parents, regardless of their training and experience, were not certified to instruct their daughter, that the necessary equipment and materials of instruction had not been secured, and that the established hours and days of instruction were not adhered to in the home instructional program.

In upholding the "home instruction" as fulfilling the requirements for compliance to the compulsory school attendance law, the court stated:

> So long as the child's education was not neglected, we think these parents, under the Constitution and laws of this state, had a right to manage and supervise the education of their child, if done in a fitting and proficient manner. The proof is not at all convincing that the education of this child was being in any way neglected. It seems to us that the state misconstrued the scope and spirit of the statute upon which the prosecution was based. (*Id.* at 180)

Equivalency a factor.—Some state compulsory school attendance laws permit home instruction as fulfilling the attendance requirement — providing the home instruction is equivalent to instruction available in public or private schools. In rare instances, where this factor is litigated, some courts ignore virtually all other factors and base their decision solely upon academic equivalency. A case in point (*State* v. *Massa*, 95 N.J. Super. 382, 231 A.2d 252, 1967) arose in New Jersey where parents were charged and convicted by the Pequannock Township Municipal Court for failing to send their child to a public school or to a private school. They insisted on providing home instruction instead, for the following stated reasons:

> Mrs. Massa said her motive was that she desired the pleasure of seeing her daughter's mind develop. She felt she wanted to be with her child when the child would be more alive and fresh. She also maintained that in school much time was wasted and that at home a student can make better use of her time. (*Id.* at 253)

Mrs. Massa introduced a number of exhibits produced by the daughter, scores on standardized tests, and other evidence which convinced the court that the instruction at home was effective in attaining academic results at least equivalent to that which could have been attained in a public or private school.

Evidence that the mother was a high school graduate and the father an interior decorator, neither of whom possessed a teacher's certificate, did not influence the court's decision. To the court, the sole issue was one of academic equivalency. Even the possible lack of social experiences such as might be provided by association with a number of classmates was discounted by the court.

The court took the stand that "all children shall be educated, not that they shall be educated in a particular way." That contention was corroborated by quoting an excerpt from an earlier Illinois case: "The law is not made to punish those who provide their children with instruction equal or superior to that obtained in public schools. It is made for the parent who fails or refuses to properly educate his child."

The court summed up its reasons for reversing the lower court's ruling in its concluding statement:

> It is the opinion of this court that defendant's daughter has received and is receiving an education equivalent to that in the Pequannock public schools. There is no indication of bad faith, or improper motive on defendant's part. Under a more definite statute with sufficient guidelines or a lesser burden of proof, this might not necessarily be the case. However, within the framework of the existing law and the nature of the stipulations by the State, this court finds the defendant not guilty and reverses the municipal court conviction. (*Id.* at 257)

As indicated in the preceding case, *State* v. *Massa*, compulsory school attendance requirements may sometimes be satisfied by home instruction — providing the home instruction is "equivalent" to that afforded by a public school of the district. But according to some jurisdictions home instruction *cannot* be "equivalent" to that of public school instruction in *social* development of the child.

In an applicable case (*Stephens* v. *Bongart*, 15 N.J. Misc. 80, 189 A. 131, 1937) the parents of two boys, ages eleven and twelve, withdrew their children from public school and instituted a program of home instruction. State authorities then charged the parents with a violation of the state's compulsory school attendance law and brought them before the court.

Among the deficiencies found in the home instruction program was that it lacked the ability to develop attitudes and to create a social setting so that children might be trained to deal with their playmates and friends as a part of a social group. After pointing to the great value of social training, Judge Seigler declared:

> I incline to the opinion that education is no longer concerned merely with the acquisition of facts; the instilling of worthy habits, attitudes, appreciations, and skills is far more important than mere imparting of subject-matter. A primary objective of education to-day is the development of character and good citizenship. Education must impart to the child the way to live. This brings me to the belief that, in a cosmopolitan area such as we live in, with all the complexities of life, and our reliance upon others to carry out the functions of education, it is almost impossible for a child to be adequately taught in his home. I cannot conceive how a child can receive in the home instruction and experiences and group activity and in social outlook in any manner or form comparable to that provided in the public school. (*Id.* at 137)

§ 2.3. Exemptions from compulsory attendance.

Courts usually uphold state laws requiring attendance at school unless the parent can show that family illness, dire financial circumstances, or some other conditions within the home are such that the child's attendance at school would endanger the well-being of, or work an undue hardship upon the family or certain of its members. Consequently attendance is sometimes waived where it is evidenced that the child is needed for services in the home. The reasons, however, must be valid and not subterfuge.

Religious objections. — In an illustrative case (*Commonwealth* v. *Smoker*, 177 Pa. Super. 435, 110 A.2d 740, 1955), testimony revealed that a parent, contending the compulsory school attendance law was in conflict with the First and Fourteenth Amendments of the United States Constitution, refused his son's attendance to school because of religious belief which prevents parents of Amish faith from sending their children to public school. On the basis of preceding court cases with similar allegations this reason for absence from school was quickly declared invalid.

The parent also filed for a farm work permit for his son on the ground that "it was necessary for him to be at home to help with the work, and take care of defendant's sick father." Had these alleged facts been true, the boy's absence from school might have been permitted. The Superintendent of Public Instruction, however, denied the permit on the ground that there was an older son available for the purposes stated.

The court upheld the Superintendent's refusal to grant the permit, stating that he was an administrative officer properly "invested with a reasonable amount of discretion in determining individual fact situations and in issuing rules to govern his administration." And in support of the Superintendent's action, the court concluded: "Undue hardship to a given family is an eminently reasonable restriction to the approval of an exemption. To issue permits merely on the convenience of a family or because of a different religious belief would result in subversion of the intent of the legislature in requiring school attendance." (*Id.* at 741)

Mental or physical disabilities. — There are numerous valid reasons for which an individual may be exempt from the compulsory school attendance law. For example, a parent may not be required to send his child to school when its mental or physical condition may endanger its well-being. An illustrative case (*State* v. *Jackson*, 71 N.H. 552, 53 A. 1021, 1902) arose in New Hampshire in 1902. In this case the parent was charged with violation of the compulsory school attendance law because he kept his 10-year-old daughter out of school for reason of feeble health as attested by a physician's testimony. Although a lower court did not exonerate the parent, the Supreme Court of New Hampshire did by reversing the lower court decision.

The stated reasoning of the higher court has served as a guiding legal principle through the years: "For the diffusion of knowledge and learning through the community, the legislature have the undoubted right, as against the mere will and pleasure of the parent, to require him to send his child to school; but they cannot repeal the natural, common-law and constitutional right of the parent to do whatever apparently is reasonably necessary to be done in defense of the life of his child." (*Id.* at 1023)

It is unlikely that this case would ever have been litigated or that the board would have objected to keeping the child from school had the parent sought the consent of the school authorities. But even though the consent of the school board was not properly sought by way of formal application, the State Supreme Court did not believe the board could act arbitrarily in the matter as is indicated by the following statement: "To require a parent whose child was confined in bed during the year to apply for and secure an excuse, would be an idle formality. Such was not the purpose or intent of the law." (*Id.* at 1024)

Special schools. — The states usually establish special schools for children whose inabilities prevent them from optimal educational progress in the regular schools. Numerous cases have arisen where parents refused to send their handicapped children to the special schools, and have thereby violated the compulsory school attendance law. One of the earliest of such cases (*State v. Ghrist*, 222 Iowa 1069, 270 N.W. 376, 1936) reaching a court of record was in Iowa in 1936. Here a child, the victim of infantile paralysis, was obviously unable to make reasonable progress in the regular public schools. The parents, nevertheless, wanted the child to attend the regular school and refused to send it to the assigned special school. Their objections were based largely upon the fact that pupils in attendance at a special school for handicapped children were frequently the victims of ridicule by other children.

The court, nevertheless, held that since the child obviously lacked the ability to meet the standards of the regular school, and that in refusing to send their child to the special school, where the best interest of the pupil could be served, the parents had violated the compulsory school attendance law.

In support of its ruling, the court stated:

> There was evident inability on the part of the child to meet the standards of the graded schools. It is in the record that he was an unfortunate victim of infantile paralysis, and that he suffers continually from pain. True, the child is sensitive and it was the fear of defendant that, being compelled to attend the Franklin School, the child might become embittered against attending any school on account of the fact that children in the graded schools were inclined to refer to the Franklin School as the "dumb school" and to treat discourteously the pupils attending. . . . From the entire record, there does not appear unreasonableness such as would warrant holding that the board exceeded the authority intended to be granted to school boards to determine where pupils may attend school. (*Id.* at 379)

Mental superiority. — There have been numerous instances in which parents have withheld public school attendance of their children whose *mental disabilities* were such as to prevent them from maximum development. It is rare, however, that parents protest the compulsory school attendance laws on the grounds that their children would be handicapped, by attending a public school, because of their alleged *mental superiority*. Nevertheless one such case (*In re Shinn*, 195 Cal. App. 2d 683, 16 Cal. Rptr. 165, 1961) did develop in California in 1961.

The parents of three children involved in this case violated the compulsory school attendance law of the state, but offered several defenses — among them, the claim that their children were of superior mental capacity, that they had advanced beyond educational achievement level of other children of similar age and grade, and that they could better realize their potential outside the public school. The court held that these claims did not constitute a sufficient excuse for nonattendance at a public school.

The court admitted that "there must be certain necessary exemptions to the compulsory education law" which would excuse the attendance at public school of those children whose mental and physical conditions prevent or render it inadvisable for them to attend school. The court concluded, however, that: "It does not appear that it was intended the Education Code, section 12152, applied to children of superior intelligence and that they should be exempted from school attendance. . . . At any rate, the question of exemption was one for the determination of the proper school authorities and not by the parents." (*Id.* at 172)

Distance of school from home. — Some states have exemption clauses in their compulsory school attendance laws which exempt a child of school age from school attendance if living further away from school than that for which free transportation is legally allowed. An illustrative case (*Villarreal* v. *State* (Tex.), 429 S.W.2d 659, 1968) is one which was adjudicated in Texas where the compulsory school attendance law has a clause which exempts "any child living more than two and one-half miles by direct and traveled road from the nearest public school supported for children of the same race and color of such child with no transportation provided."

In this case a mother filed an appeal from a judgment of the Juvenile Court in which the trial judge found that her daughter was a truant and therefore a delinquent child. The mother contended that the judgment should be reversed because the child had been placed by school authorities in a school which was more than two and one-half miles from her home.

There was contradictory evidence as to whether or not the disputed distance was actually more than two and one-half miles. Moreover, there was some evidence that showed there was another school, other than the one to which the student had been assigned, that was only two miles from the girl's home. Her mother claimed that she was unaware of the existence of such school or that it may have been nearer.

On the basis of the evidence, the Court of Civil Appeals of Texas affirmed the judgment of the trial court which found that the "student did not come within exemption to statute... that child was a truant and therefore a delinquent child." (*Id.* at 659)

§ 2.4. Vaccination as a condition for attendance.

In the early stages of laws requiring compulsory school attendance, as well as vaccination of pupils, there was conflict of opinions as to whether a parent was guilty of violating the compulsory school attendance law if his child was sent to school but denied admission therein by reasons of not having complied with the vaccination requirement. At first the courts applied a strict construction to the compulsory school law, holding that parents must send their children to school, but having done that, regardless of the fact that the children were denied admission for failure to comply with the valid vaccination regulations, the parent had fulfilled the requirement of the compulsory school attendance law and could not be convicted for violation of the vaccination requirement.

This judicial reasoning, however, was short lived. Beginning with a New York case in 1914 (*People* v. *Ekerold*, 211 N.Y. 386, 105 N.E. 670, 1914) the early trend was reversed, and since that time the courts have generally held that parents are guilty of violating the compulsory school attendance laws even when the children are sent to school but denied admission because of failure to meet vaccination requirements. In *People* v. *Ekerold*, the court based its decision on legislative intent rather than on strict construction of the statute. The court pointed out that it was readily apparent that the legislature, in passing one law requiring compulsory school attendance, and in passing another requiring vaccination as a condition for admission, did not intend that one should be used as an excuse to disobey the other.

In explaining the logic for its decision the court stated:

> It is hardly to be assumed that when the Legislature passed the later statute there had slipped from its theoretical mind remembrance of the other law providing a very important condition of attendance at public schools, and, if it had purposed that a child might be excused from attendance by reason of the unwillingness of its parent to have it vaccinated, I cannot but believe that something would have been said on that subject.

> It does not require much spirit of prophecy to foresee what will follow a contrary construction of the statute. If a parent may escape all obligation under the statute requiring him to send his children to school by simply alleging that he does not believe in vaccination, the policy of the state to give some education to all children, if necessary by compelling measures, will become more or less a farce under existing legislation. (*Id.* at 672)

Religious objections. — The majority of cases evolving from violation of the compulsory school attendance laws where vaccination is a mandated condition for attendance are based upon religious beliefs. A case in point (*Anderson* v. *State*, 84 Ga. App. 259, 65 S.E.2d 848, 1951) arose in Georgia in 1951. Some of the facts of the case indicated that (1) the county nurse attempted to vaccinate the children against certain contagious diseases; (2) the defendant parents objected to the vaccination of the children on the ground that it was against their religious beliefs; (3) the parents believed in divine healing through faith rather than taking vaccine or immunization against disease; (4) the children returned to school but were denied admission for non-compliance with the vaccination requirement; and (5) the court then held the parents guilty for violating the compulsory school attendance law of the state.

In commenting on the pertinent facts of the case the court concluded:

> Liberty of conscience is one thing. License to endanger the lives of others by practice contrary to statutes passed for the public safety and in reliance upon modern medical knowledge is another. ... The defendants in this case sought to comply with their duty to send their children to school but at the same time usurp the prerogative of the school authorities, and also undertook to fix the rules under which they should attend. Their contention therefore that they did actually enroll the children unvaccinated constitutes no valid defense. ... Such a contention is unsound for the reason that an offer to do a thing only upon waiver of the conditions precedent thereto amounts to no offer at all. (*Id.* at 852)

Defiance of statutes requiring vaccination as a condition for admission to the public schools is sometimes expressed more vigorously than by just merely refusing to have the children vaccinated. For example, in an Arkansas case in 1964 (*Cude* v. *State*, 237 Ark. 927, 377 S.W.2d 816, 1964) parents not only refused to have their children vaccinated, but refused to accept them back into the home if they should be vaccinated.

In ruling upon this case the court was unanimous in agreeing that refusal to comply with the compulsory

school attendance law was in violation of a constitutional provision which was interpreted as meaning that
"anyone has the right to worship God in the manner of
his own choice, but that it does not mean that he can engage in religious practices inconsistent with the peace,
safety and health of the inhabitants of the State, and it
does not mean that parents, on religious grounds, have
the right to deny their children an education." (*Id.* at
818-19)

However, with regard to the granting of a petition
which ordered that the children be removed from the
custody of the parents and placed under the care and
direction of local juvenile authorities until such time as
suitable homes could be found for them, the court was
not unanimous as evidenced by the opinion of a dissenting judge: "I as a judge am not willing now or ever to
say as a matter of law that the failure to comply with
one simple regulation of school administrative authorities constitutes such neglect of children as to warrant
the state administering the cruel and unusual punishment of depriving such children of their natural parents and depriving the natural parents of their children." (*Id.* at 821)

Statutory exemption. — It is unusual for a state statute to exempt a parent from compliance with the vaccination requirement of his child as a condition for
school attendance merely because of religious beliefs.
Such a statute, however, does exist for the state of
North Carolina. With reference to the vaccination requirement, the North Carolina statute (G.S. 130-93.1,
h) stipulates: "This article should not apply to children

whose parent, parents, or guardian are bona fide members of a recognized religious organization whose teachings are contrary to the practices herein required, and no certificate for admission to any private, public or parochial school shall be required."

It is also unusual that such a statute would receive judicial sanction, since the general legal principle is that "the freedom to believe as one chooses in the matter of religion is absolute, but the freedom to act in the exercise of religion is subject to regulation in the public interest and for the good order of society."

In the instant case (*State* v. *Miday*, 263 N.C. 747, 140 S.E.2d 325, 1965) the parent did not have his child vaccinated because of conflict with religious convictions. Consequently the child was sent home from school for failure to comply with the legal requirement of vaccination.

The Supreme Court ruled in favor of the parent by reversing a decision of a lower court which had convicted the parent for violation of the compulsory school attendance law. In the final ruling the Court said:

> With respect to the defendant's conviction for failing to send his child to school as required by G. S. 115-166, it appears that the defendant did everything within his power to keep his child in school except to waive what he believed to be his rights under G.S. 130-93.1(h). So long as the defendant, in good faith, was asserting his rights as he conceived them under the statute, in our opinion he was not subject to conviction. (*Id.* at 329)

Another case (*McCartney* v. *Austin*, 57 Misc. 2d 525, 293 N.Y.S.2d 188, 1968) was similar to *State* v. *Miday* in several respects. There was, however, one decisive difference. In the *Miday* case, the parent was exempted from having his child vaccinated by virtue of a clause which exempted those who belonged to a religious organization (Miracle Revival Fellowship) whose teachings were in opposition to vaccinations and immunizations. In the instant case, *McCartney* v. *Austin*, there was reported a similar exemption clause which could be used as a defense. But the plaintiff's faith (Roman Catholic) "does not have any proscription against inoculation."

The disputed section of the New York Public Health Law is as follows: "Every person in parental relation to a child in this state shall have administered to such child an adequate dose or doses of an immunizing agent against poliomyelitis. . . . This section shall not apply to children whose parent, parents, or guardian are bona fide members of a recognized religious organization whose teachings are contrary to the practices herein required. . . ." (*Id.* at 190)

The court dispensed with the case in the following manner: "This court concludes that section 2164 of the Public Health Law does not interfere with plaintiff's freedom of worship, that it is not discriminatory nor does it constitute an establishment of a religion, and that it is constitutional and binding upon plaintiffs." (*Id.* at 200)

§ 2.5. Desegregation and compulsory attendance.

Very few of the numerous court cases involving desegregation of the races in the public schools refer directly to compulsory school attendance requirements. In some instances, however, where discrimination is alleged, in the assignment of pupils, a parent may refuse to send his child to an "inferior" school and thereby be charged with violation of the compulsory school attendance law.

A case (*Dobbins* v. *Commonwealth*, 198 Va. 697, 96 S.E.2d 154, 1957) in point arose in Virginia in 1957, when the parents of a Negro child failed to send their child to a Negro school, after permission to attend a white school instead was denied by the board of education. Instead of sending his daughter to the assigned Negro school, the father presented her to the white high school where the physical facilities and educational opportunities were admittedly superior to those of the Negro school. As a consequence the child attended no school at all, and the father was accordingly charged with violation of the compulsory school attendance law. He pleaded not guilty but was found guilty by a lower court. The Supreme Court of Appeals, however, reversed the lower court ruling and said:

> Accused did not refuse to send his child to school but sought to have her attend. The school board's refusal to admit her solely because of her race to the school attended by children of the white race similarly situated and the resultant requirement that Dobbins send her to a school of materially poorer facilities and educational advantages on penalty of prosecution was an unconstitutional application of [the compulsory school attendance law] and a denial to him of equal protection of the law guaranteed by the Fourteenth Amendment of the Constitution of the United States . . . [the com-

pulsory school attendance law] cannot be applied as a coercive means to require a citizen to forego or relinquish her constitutional rights. (*Id.* at 156-157)

Since *pupil placement* determines where a pupil may or may not attend school, it is closely related to the issue of compulsory and prohibitory school attendance. Prior to the *Brown* decision of 1954, pupil placement was not a very litigious issue; school officials were generally permitted to exercise their discretion in placing pupils in schools according to their needs and the facilities of the school district. Despite the *Brown* decision, many school boards continued to assign pupils to schools in such a manner as to perpetuate segregated schools. Obviously the placement of pupils in particular schools because of race or color was in conflict with constitutional law as interpreted by the United States Supreme Court. Nevertheless, states continued to enact pupil placement laws. Those which were allegedly designed to circumvent the court ruling were challenged in the federal courts, where they were consistently declared unconstitutional.

Notwithstanding the unconstitutionality of laws which prevented desegregation of the races in the public schools, numerous school boards adopted various pupil placement plans which perpetuated, to some degree, the dual school system. The "all deliberate speed" mandate, in many instances, became "too deliberate" to please certain school patrons, and, consequently, an avalanche of court cases descended upon the Federal Courts of Appeals, where considerable "gradualism" had been permitted for local school boards to convert their dual school systems to unitary systems, within which no person would be excluded from any school because of race or color.

The issue finally reached a climax when a case (*Alexander* v. *Holmes County Board of Education* (Miss.), 90 S. Ct. 29, 1969) where, on writ of certiorari to the United States Court of Appeals for the Fifth Circuit, the Supreme Court remanded the case to the lower court which "shall retain jurisdiction to insure prompt compliance with its order." The terse statement of the Supreme Court follows:

> The question presented is one of paramount importance, involving as it does the denial of fundamental rights to many thousands of school children who are presently attending Mississippi schools under segregated conditions contrary to the applicable decisions of this Court. Against this background the Court of Appeals should have denied all motions for additional time because continued operation of segregated schools under a standard of allowing "all deliberate speed" for desegregation is no longer constitutionally permissible. Under explicit holdings of this Court the obligation of every school district is to terminate dual school systems at once and to operate now and hereafter only unitary schools. (*Id.* at 29)

Whereas the United States Supreme Court may order immediate termination of school attendance practices which perpetuate segregation of the races in the public schools, the lower federal courts are saddled with the difficult task of devising means whereby the desegregation might be accomplished. The two most common methods proposed by the federal courts to correct racial imbalance of attendance in the public schools are (1) rezoning attendance districts and (2) cross-busing pupils.

Many parents, as well as some high-ranking governmental officials, vigorously protest having children transported great distances just to promote a racial balance of pupil attendance. Consequently court orders for the mass busing of pupils are subject to judicial review. For example, on March 16, 1970, the Supreme Court *granted a delay* in a busing schedule ordered by the Fourth Circuit Court of Appeals for the Charlotte-Mecklenburg County, North Carolina schools.

The following reference to the case (*The New York Times*, Tuesday, March 17, 1970, p. 20) indicates that the issue is far from being permanently resolved:

> The Supreme Court declined today to disturb a lower court's grant to officials in Charlotte, N.C., of a delay in implementing a pupil desegregation plan. There was no dissent.

The purpose of the delay, which was initially ordered by the United States Court of Appeals for the Fourth Circuit, is to permit Federal District Judge James P. McMillan of Charlotte to hear evidence on conflicting contentions as to the impact of his own busing order.

Under his order, school officials were required to achieve a racial balance of about 71 percent white students and 29 percent Negroes in 100 of the districts 103 schools.

The plan, which was worked out by computers, paired suburban white schools with Negro schools in the central city and called for cross busing of students for distances of up to 15 miles.

School officials contended that many students would spend as much as two and a half hours a day on buses. They said that 526 new buses would be required, that the community lacked the $3.5 million needed to buy them, and that the buses could not be found on such short notice.

§ 2.6. Dual enrolment as a complicating factor.

Although the issue as to whether or not participation in a dual enrolment program is a violation of the compulsory school attendance law, has not been litigated often, there are a couple of cases which are applicable. One of the cases (*Morton* v. *Board of Education of City of Chicago*, 69 Ill. App. 2d 38, 216 N.E.2d 305, 1966) evolved from an experimental program conducted in the City of Chicago. Here students who were enrolled in private schools were also enrolled part time in a public high school. Students took all of their courses in the public school except English, social studies, music and art which were taken at a nearby private school.

The legality of the Chicago dual enrolment program was challenged on the ground that it permitted the parents of participating students to violate the compulsory attendance law of Illinois. The applicable law stipulates: "Whoever has custody or control of any child between the ages of 7 and 16 years shall cause such child to attend some public school in the district wherein the child resides the entire time it is in session during the regular school term." The law exempts a child from attending a *public* school if he is attending a private or parochial school.

After considering arguments by the litigants concerning alleged violation of the compulsory school attendance law, the trial court found that the dual enrolment plan did not violate the statutory provisions, and ordered that the complaint be dismissed with prejudice.

The Appellate Court of Illinois then dismissed the complaint for an injunction to restrain the school board from maintaining the "experimental" dual enrolment plan wherein children enrolled part time in a public school and part time in a nonpublic school. The Appellate Court concluded:

> Since the object of the compulsory attendance law is that all children be educated and not that they be educated in any particular manner or place, part time enrollment in a nonpublic school is permitted by Section 26-1, so long as the child receives a complete education. (*Id.* at 308)

The laws of some states are rather specific in requiring that enrolment be restricted to *one* school during the regular school period. For example, as was reported in a 1966 case (*Special District for the Education and Training of Handicapped Children* v. *Wheeler* (Mo.), 408 S.W.2d 60, 1966) the statutes of Missouri stipulate: "Every parent, guardian or other person in this state having charge, control or custody of a child between the ages of seven and sixteen years shall cause the child to attend regularly some day school, public, private, parochial or parish."

Nothing in the statute indicated that the compulsory

attendance law could be met by dividing attendance at more than *one* school. Therefore when a public school provided speech therapy for parochial school children released from school for part of their regular six-hour day in violation of the statute, the practice was declared by the court to be invalid. According to a statement of the court there was nothing in the decision aimed against nonpublic school students:

> The Attorney General contends the condemnation of the practice here in question by the trial court is unconstitutional because it deprives nonpublic school pupils of liberty without due process of law and equal protection of the laws. There is no merit in this contention. The fact that parochial school students, not public school students, are involved here, is incidental. There is nothing in the record to indicate the trial court invoked the compulsory attendance law because the students were parochial school students and not public school students. (*Id.* at 64)

§ 2.7. Attendance status of married girls.

Compelling attendance of married girls. — The legal principle that married girls could not be compelled to attend school has been firmly — and likely permanently — established. In the first case (*State* v. *Priest*, 210 La. 389, 27 So. 2d 173, 1946) involving this issue, a 15-year-old married girl contested the legality of a school regulation and a juvenile court order to attend a school. In supporting the girl's complaint, the Louisiana State Supreme Court ruled that "marriage" "emancipates" a minor female and accordingly releases her from the compulsory school attendance laws.

Responding to the claim that the marriage was unlawful due to violation of the legal age limits for marriage in Louisiana, the court stated: ". . . such marriage once performed becomes a valid and legal marriage (if there are no legal impediments other than age), and that the female minor thus married enjoys the status of a wife and has a right to live at the matrimonial domicile of her husband and is no longer under the control of her parents." (*Id.* at 174)

A strikingly similar case (*In re State in Interest of Goodwin*, 214 La. 1062, 39 So. 2d 731, 1949) dealing with same issue was adjudicated just three years later in the same state of Louisiana. Here a 14-year-old married girl denied that absence from school contributed to truancy in her case and argued that she should not be required to attend school as ordered by a lower court. On appeal to the State Supreme Court, it was again ruled that the girl could not legally be required to attend school, by virtue of the fact that she was "irrevocably emancipated."

As in the preceding case, the court disregarded the claim of an illegal under-age marriage and declared:

> Consequently, Clydell is irrevocably emancipated by this marriage as a matter of right. And although until she reaches the age of 18 she is not relieved of all of the disabilities that attach to minority of this emancipation, she is relieved of parental control and, as was held in the *Priest* case, is no longer amenable to the compulsory school attendance law of this state. . . . (*Id.* at 733)

Prohibiting attendance of married girls. — In direct contrast to those cases where school boards attempt to *compel* school attendance of married girls, there are cases in which school board regulations are designed to *prohibit* school attendance of married girls. The earliest case (*McLeod* v. *State*, 154 Miss. 468, 122 So. 737, 1929), in point arose in Mississippi where a 15-year-old married girl was denied admission to a school by the school board for the alleged claim that "married students are detrimental to the good government and usefulness of the school." This claim was forcefully set aside by the court as is revealed in the following declaration:

> It is argued that marriage emancipates a child from all parental control of its conduct, as well as such control by the school authorities; and that the marriage relation brings about views of life which should not be known to unmarried children; that a married child in the public schools will make known to its associates in schools such views, which will therefore be detrimental to the welfare of the school. We fail to appreciate the force of the argument. Marriage is a domestic relation highly favored by law. When the relation is entered into with correct motives, the effect on the husband and wife is refining and elevating, rather than demoralizing. Pupils associating in school with a child occupying such a relation, it seems, would be benefited instead of harmed. And, furthermore, it is commendable in married persons of school age to desire to further pursue their education, and thereby become better fitted for the duties of life. And they are as much subject to the rules of the school as unmarried pupils, and punishable to the same extent for a breach of such rules. (*Id.* at 738-39)

During the same year as the *McLeod* case, a somewhat similar case (*Nutt* v. *Board of Education of Goodland*, 128 Kan. 507, 278 P. 1065, 1928) was adjudicated in the state of Kansas. In the instant case, a school board denied readmission of a married girl who had left school temporarily. Apparently the main reason for the board's refusal to readmit the girl was because of alleged immorality. She had given birth to a child conceived out of wedlock, but was married before the child was born. The court voided the school board action and declared:

> The fact that the plaintiff's daughter desired to attend school was of itself an indication of character warranting favorable consideration. Other than the fact that she had a child conceived out of wedlock, no sufficient reason is advanced for preventing her from attending school. Her child was born in wedlock, and the fact that her husband may have abandoned her should not prevent her from gaining an education which would better fit her to meet the problems of life. (*Id.* at 1066)

Much more recently, the legal principle that a girl cannot be permanently denied a legal education because of marriage was substantiated by a Texas case (*Alvin Independent School District* v. *Cooper* (Tex. Civ. App.), 404 S.W.2d 76, 1966) which involved a 16-year-old girl who, in her sophomore year in high school, was married and withdrew from school. Subsequently a child was born to the marriage. The girl divorced her husband and sought readmission to the high school. In the meantime the school board formulated a rule designed to permanently exclude such persons from school with the assertion that "A pupil who marries can no longer be considered a youth. By the very act of getting married, he or she becomes an adult and assumes the responsibility of adulthood. . . . If a married pupil wants to start her family, she must withdraw from public school." (*Id.* at 77)

In voiding the board's rule, the court stated:

> The practical and legal effect is that appellee is deprived of a legal education, except as she might obtain it at her own expense in a private or parochial school. . . . We are of the view that appellants were without legal authority to adopt the rule or policy that excludes the mother of a child from admission to the school if she is of the age for which the State furnishes school funds. (*Id.* at 77)

§ 2.8. Attendance status of unwed mothers.

The issue concerning the eligibility of a young mother to attend school was litigated again in 1969. There was, however, one significant different factor in the latter case (*Perry* v. *Grenada Municipal Separate School District* (Miss.), 300 F. Supp. 748, 1969); the two young mothers involved in the case *were not married*, either before or after the birth of a child.

The school board denied admission, and as a consequence, action was brought against the school district by the two unwed mothers who asserted that the school board's policy of excluding unwed mothers from high school admission violated the due process and equal protection clauses of the Fourteenth Amendment.

The District Court "held that unwed mothers could not be excluded from high schools of the district for sole reason that they were unwed mothers . . . unless on a fair hearing before the school authorities they were found to be so lacking in moral character that their presence in the schools would taint the education of other students." (*Id.* at 748)

Excerpts from the District Court's opinion manifest the judicial compassion toward the girls:

> Certainly school officials recognize the importance of education and the effect of a rigid rule which forever bars an individual from obtaining an education . . . after the girl has the child, she should have the opportunity for applying for readmission and demonstrating to the school that she is qualified to continue her education. . . . Without a high school education, the individual is ill equipped for life, and is prevented from seeking higher education.

> The Court would like to make manifestly clear that lack of moral character is certainly a reason for excluding a child from public education. But the fact that a girl has one child out of wedlock does not forever brand her as a scarlet woman undeserving of any chance for rehabilitation or the opportunity for future education. (*Id.* at 753)

Chapter 3

AUTHORITY OVER CURRICULAR ACTIVITIES

§ 3.0. Generally.

As indicated in the preceding chapter, children within specified age limits, are required to attend a public school, a private school or an approved home school. School attendance, however, does not in itself insure an education for the pupil. In fact nothing can insure an education for those who refuse it. Although the term is frequently used there is no such thing as "compulsory education." The state may compel attendance but whether or not the pupil receives an education will depend upon his willingness, with parental consent, to engage in the activities and experiences which the school provides. The best the school can do is to provide an environment and activities conducive to learning. In so doing, it is well for school officials to consider

45

relative authority of the school and the home in curricular matters.

Allocation of legal authority over the curriculum is often the subject of dispute and litigation. However it is generally agreed that within constitutional limits, the legislature is empowered to determine the types and contents of curricula and the manner of their control.

In rare instances state constitutions provide for specific inclusions in the curriculum, and to that extent preempt statutory enactments on those items provided for in the constitution. For example, the constitution of Louisiana requires "instruction upon the constitutional system of the state and national government, and the duties of citizenship." The Utah constitution requires "teaching of the metric system." Conversely, several states have in their constitutions certain prohibitive provisions such as those outlawing sectarian instruction.

Virtually every state has enacted legislation requiring certain subject matters to be included in the public school curriculum. Illustrative provisions are those that prescribe instruction in the United States Constitution, the state constitution, American history, civics, citizenship, health habits, driver education, and, more recently, sex education. Most of the statutes pertaining to the curriculum and its administration are rather general — as they should be — with delegated authority to local boards or professional personnel to determine the specifics.

In numerous instances pupils and their parents object to certain state and local requirements pertaining to curricular activities. The objections are frequently so severe as to foment litigation. Then the courts must decide if the curricula requirements are in accord with statutory provisions, or, in many instances, if the statutes themselves are within constitutional limits. In essence, then, the judiciary plays an important role in determining the legal prescriptions, prohibitions, and compulsions of the school curriculum.

References to following court cases indicate circumstances which influence the courts in determining relative authority of the parent and the school concerning curricular issues and their application to the pupils.

§ 3.1. Prescribing school subjects.

Singing lessons. — Early court cases indicate that state judiciaries followed rather closely the old common law whereby "the home is considered the keystone of governmental structure" and "parents rule supreme during the minority of their children." This is illustrated in a case (*School Board District No. 18* v. *Thompson*, 24 Okla. 1, 103 P. 578, 1909) where parents succeeded by mandamus action to compel school authorities to reinstate their children in the public schools, from which they were expelled for their refusal, at their parents' direction, to take singing lessons, which constituted part of the prescribed course of study.

The basic question involved in this case was "whether a patron of the public schools may make a reasonable selection from a course of study prescribed by the proper school authorities for his child to pursue, in opposition to a rule prescribed by such authorities requiring the child to take all the studies in such course." (*Id.* at 578)

Ruling in favor of the parents, the court emphasized the limited authority of school officials in curricular prescriptions: "To our mind the right of the board of education to prescribe the course of study and designate the text-books to be used does not carry with it the absolute power to require the pupils to study all of the branches prescribed in the course in opposition to the parents reasonable wishes in relation to some of them." (*Id.* at 579)

In conclusion the court made reference to the respective authority of state and parent over the pupil in regard to various school matters:

> The school authorities of the state have the power to classify and grade the scholars in their respective districts and cause them to be taught in such departments as they may deem expedient. They may also prescribe the courses of study and text-books for the use of the schools, and such reasonable rules and regulations as they may think needful. They may also require prompt attendance, respectful deportment, and diligence in study. The parent, however, has a right to make a reasonable selection from the prescribed course of study for his child to pursue, as the right of the parent in that regard is superior to that of the school officers and the teachers. (*Id.* at 582)

Domestic science. — In an early Nebraska case (*Kelley* v. *Ferguson*, 95 Neb. 63, 144 N.W. 1039, 1914) a legal principle denoting the school board's limited scope of authority over the curriculum was established when the Nebraska Supreme Court ruled against a school board which refused a request of a parent to excuse his daughter from studying domestic science. The request was made because to pursue the study of the subject would have necessitated considerable travel to the building where the subject was taught and back to the regular school where the rule required pupils to be for dismissal. In support of its ruling the court stated:

> The public school is one of the main bulwarks of our nation, and we would not knowingly do anything to undermine it; but we should be careful to avoid permitting our love for this noble institution to cause us to regard it as "all in all" and destroy both the God-given and constitutional right of a parent to have some voice in the bringing up and education of his children. . . . (*Id.* at 1043)

> The state is more and more taking hold of the private affairs of individuals and requiring that they conduct their business affairs honestly and with due regard for the public good. All this is commendable and must receive sanction of every good citizen. But in this age of agitation, such as the world has never known before, we want to be careful lest we carry the doctrine of governmental paternalism too far, for after all is said and done, the prime factor in our scheme of government is the American home. (*Id.* at 1044)

Physical education. — Some decades ago parents began to object to inclusions in the curriculum other than "book learning." This was particularly true where the curricular activities were in opposition to religious standards of the parents. Litigation frequently arose as a result of certain activities in the physical education program. For example, in a California case (*Hardwick* v. *Board of Trustees*, 54 Cal. App. 696, 205 P. 49, 1921) it was revealed that parents requested their children to be excused from dancing as a part of physical education on the grounds that "such exercise was offensive to the conscientious scruples and contrary to the religious beliefs and principles" of the children and their parents. They were particularly opposed to those dances "where the arms of the children, as they danced with the opposite sex, were clasped around and about the shoulders of their dancing partners."

The request of the parents was denied and the pupils expelled because of refusal to participate. Although the court held the school authorities had no right to expel the children for their refusal to take part in the dancing, the court upheld the right of the schools to include dancing in the curriculum.

A brief excerpt of the court's rather lengthy discourse on the case indicates judicial opinion as to the school's scope of authority concerning curricular activities:

> To the end that the public school system may in full measure function according to its purposes, there must, of course, be rules and regulations for the government thereof, and these the Legislature has either directly provided or has vested the school authorities with plenary power to establish and, quite naturally and with eminent propriety, has committed to said authorities the right and power to prescribe the courses of study to be followed in the various grades of the system and to maintain at all times the discipline indispensably necessary

to the successful prosecution of the high purpose thereof.... (*Id.* at 51)

Another case (*Mitchell* v. *McCall*, 273 Ala. 604, 143 So. 2d 629, 1962) concerning participation in physical education classes was adjudicated more recently. Here a girl refused to engage in the activities of the physical education class because the costumes worn were, in her opinion, "immodest and sinful." Even though the school authorities permitted the girl to wear such costume as she desired and to engage in only such activities as she considered appropriate for the costume chosen, her father objected to the girl's being in the class. He contended that the wearing of the different clothes than those prescribed would make the girl stand out as a "speckled bird" and "subject to the contumely of her fellow students."

In response to this contention the court stated:

All citizens insofar as they hold views different from the majority of their fellows are subject to such inconveniences. And this is especially true of those who hold religious or moral beliefs which are looked upon with disdain by the majority. It is precisely every citizen's right to be a "speckled bird" that our constitution, state and federal, seek to insure. And solace for the embarrassment that is attendant upon holding such beliefs must be found by the individual citizen in his own moral courage and strength of conviction, and not in a court of law. (*Id.* at 632)

Even though every reasonable concession was made in behalf of the parent and his daughter, the court ruled that the girl was obligated to attend the course in physical education, and maintained that the requirement did not violate her constitutional rights.

Sex education. — A very controversial issue, which is steadily growing in intensity, has to do with the inclusion of sex education in the curriculum. Judging from the literature on the subject, parents are rather evenly divided in voicing support or opposition to the propriety and legality of prescribing subject matter on sex education. Legislatures, too, are in variance. Some have enacted legislation providing for sex instruction, whereas others have enacted laws to prohibit inclusion of sex education in the curriculum. Although litigation on the issue has already begun at the lower court level, no cases by courts of record have been reported as this manuscript is being prepared. Despite the fact that the question of including sex education in the curriculum is being hotly debated, actual litigation on the issue has not been very apparent. It is likely, however, that applicable court cases will be forthcoming soon.

A suit (*TASTE, Inc.* v. *Topeka Board of Education,* Action No. 112064, December 30, 1969) which portends the onset of widespread litigation on the issue of sex education, was initiated by a Topeka, Kansas, organization in December, 1969. Reference to the suit is made in *Nolpe Notes*, February, 1970, as follows:

> Paul Clemmer, President of Truth About Sex Training in Education (TASTE), filed a suit on behalf of his organization. (The petition was subsequently amended to name Clemmer as plaintiff in lieu of TASTE.) Named defendant is the Topeka Board of Education, its officials and employees.

Under fire is the school system's "Human Growth and Development" curriculum and its materials consisting of films, printed materials and course outlines. The suit contends teaching sex education is unconstitutional for six reasons: it violates Article 1 of the 14th Amendment to the United States Constitution because it "destroys our personal and inalienable rights to liberty and happiness in that it is designed to question parental authority by encouraging analysis, appraisal and criticism of parental authority"; that parents, required to send children to the public schools, have the right under this amendment to have their children taught subjects or topics which are not "repugnant to the family," and that sex education "destroys the opportunity for the family to make its own moral and ethical value judgment on sexual behavior, sexual intercourse, pre-marital and extra-marital relations"; it violates the 9th Amendment to the United States Constitution because parents have the right to regulate what is being taught in public schools; the training is an unlawful assumption of power by the school board, because it has never been delegated by the legislature or constitution. The suit contends the power is reserved to the citizenry on the basis of the 10th Amendment to the United States Constitution; sex education is funded by ad valorem taxes and thus is unconstitutional, because the funds are being used without proper authority from the citizens, the legislature or the constitution; the school board has abused its rights of discretion in prescribing courses of study in that sex education "vitally affects the health of children, the parent-child relationship, and family structure," and because the parents do not have control over what is taught.

§ 3.2. Prohibiting the teaching of a foreign language.

The first United States Supreme Court case (*Meyer v. Nebraska*, 43 S. Ct. 625, 1923) which concerns the curriculum of a state school system originated in Nebraska. The main factor leading up to the case indicates that, after World War I, several states enacted legislation prohibiting the teaching of German to nonpublic or public school pupils who had not completed requirements of Grade VIII. It was said the purpose of the legislation was "to promote civic development by inhibiting training and education of the immature in foreign tongues and before they could learn English and acquire American ideals."

Although the courts of three states (Nebraska, Iowa, and Ohio) had sanctioned the legislation as legitimate exercise of the police power, the Supreme Court ruled that the legislation was an arbitrary interference with the liberty of parents to control and educate their children, and that it violated the liberty guaranteed by the Fourteenth Amendment. The following excerpts indicate the court's reasoning in its decision:

> ... it is the natural duty of the parent to give his children education suitable to their station in life. ...
>
> That the state may do much, go very far, indeed, in order to improve the quality of its citizens, physically, mentally and morally, is clear; but the individual has certain fundamental rights which must be respected. The protection of the Constitution extends to all, to those who speak other languages as well as those born with English on the tongue. Perhaps it would be highly advantageous

if all had ready understanding of our ordinary speech, but this cannot be coerced by methods which conflict with the Constitution — a desirable end cannot be promoted by prohibited means. (*Id.* at 627)

§ 3.3. Prohibiting the teaching of evolution.

For many years school boards, teachers, and parents have been in a quandary regarding the legality of having the theory of evolution taught in the public schools. At least three states (Arkansas, Mississippi, and Tennessee) have had "antievolution" or "monkey" laws on their statute books for several decades. Although the validity of the Mississippi law has not yet been tested in a court of record, the statute of Tennessee has been adjudicated twice in the state courts, and the Arkansas law has run the gamut of litigation all the way through the highest court in the land.

The Tennessee law was first tested in 1927 in the famous *Scopes* case (*Scopes* v. *Tennessee*, 154 Tenn. 105, 289 S.W. 363, 1927). Although this case may not have been the most significant, it was certainly one of the most spectacular in a century. As is generally known, Scopes was convicted for violating the Tennessee law for teaching in the public schools "a certain theory that denied the story of the divine creation of man, as taught in the Bible, and did teach instead thereof that man descended from a lower order of animals." (*Id.* at 363) Forty years later another suit was filed in a Tennessee court where a teacher was dismissed for teaching the evolution theory, but was reinstated after the Tennessee Legislature voted to repeal the so-called "monkey law."

The Arkansas case (*Epperson* v. *State of Arkansas*, 89 S. Ct. 266, 1968) was instituted by a teacher seeking a declaration that the Arkansas statute was void, and enjoining the State and defendant officials from dismissing her for violation of the statute which aimed to prohibit the teaching of evolution. The law was decreed unconstitutional by a chancery court in 1966. Then in 1967 the Supreme Court of Arkansas reversed the decree and held that the antievolution law is a valid exercise of the state's power to specify the curriculum in the public schools. Finally, however, the United States Supreme Court reversed the judgment of the Supreme Court of Arkansas by concluding: "Plainly, the law is contrary to the mandate of the First, and in violation of the Fourteenth Amendment to the Constitution." (*Id.* at 273)

Since the anti-evolution cases were instituted against or by teachers, there might be some question as to why they are discussed in a study designed to deal with parental versus state authority over the pupil. The reason is that, basically, the parents are the ones who are most concerned as to whether the theory of evolution should be treated in the public school curriculum. The fundamentalist conviction of parents is expressed in the following excerpt from a public appeal used in the campaign to secure adoption of the anti-evolution statute:

> Now let the mothers and fathers of our state that are trying to raise their children in the Christian faith arise in their might and vote for this anti-

evolution bill that will take it out of our tax schools. When they have saved the children they have saved the state. (*Id.* at 272)

The opposite stand on the issue is indicated by a parent who subsequently joined Epperson as an appellant in the Arkansas case because of his alleged interest in seeing that his son "be informed of scientific theories and hypotheses." (*Id.* at 273)

§ 3.4. Compelling pupils to salute the flag.

A long period of litigation in the state courts, concerning the flag salute as a requirement of the school program and as a condition for school attendance appeared to be reaching a climax when the issue reached the United States Supreme Court in a case (*Minersville School District* v. *Gobitis*, 310 U.S. 586, 1940) instigated by the Jehovah's Witnesses who protested a school board resolution requiring pupils to salute the American flag. While saluting the flag, pupils were to recite in unison a pledge of allegiance to it "and to the Republic for which it stands; one Nation indivisible, with liberty and justice for all."

The Jehovah's Witnesses protested the regulation because their religion forbids paying homage to the flag. They contended that the flag salute was unconstitutional as applied to them because their religious belief prohibits them from "bowing down before any graven image."

After receiving an adverse decision from the state courts Gobitis appealed the case to the Supreme Court which upheld the state court ruling that it was within the rights of the school board to require the flag salute as a means of achieving a feeling of national unity. Justice Frankfurter, who delivered the opinion of the court stated:

> What the school authorities are really asserting is the right to awaken in the child's mind considerations as to the significance of the flag contrary to those implanted by the parent. In such an attempt the state is normally at a disadvantage in competing with the parent's authority, as long — and this is the vital aspect of religious toleration — as parents are unmolested in their right to counteract by their own persuasiveness the wisdom and rightness to those loyalties which the state's educational system is seeking to promote. . . . (*Id.* at 599)

> The preciousness of the family relation, the authority and independence which give dignity to parenthood, indeed the enjoyment of all freedom, presuppose the kind of ordered society which is summarized by our flag. (*Id.* at 600)

Voluminous press reaction in newspapers, law reviews, and scholarly writings, expressions by the American Civil Liberties Union, the American Bar Association, and the United States Department of Justice; and the strong dissenting opinion of Justice Stone in the *Gobitis* case, all gave encouragement to the Jehovah's Witnesses to press further their opposition to the required flag salute in the public school program. They took advantage of their support by instituting another case (*West Virginia State Board of Education* v. *Barnette*, 319 U.S. 624, 1943) after the State Board of Education in West Virginia passed a resolution requiring the flag salute in all the public schools of the state.

As in the preceding cases, the constitutionality of the regulation was challenged. When the case finally reached the United States Supreme Court, the high tribunal ruled in favor of Barnette, a Jehovah's Witness, thereby reversing the decision of the *Gobitis* case.

In substance the Supreme Court held that a school board, in compelling pupils to salute and pledge allegiance to the American flag "transcends constitutional limitations on their power and invades the sphere of intellect and spirit which it is the purpose of the First Amendment to our Constitution to reserve from all official control." (*Id.* at 642)

The court was by no means unanimous in the ruling decision for this case; three of the justices dissented. The dissent of Justice Frankfurter was especially severe and considerably lengthier than that of the majority opinion. After granting that "parents have the privilege of choosing which schools they wish their children to attend" he questioned "whether the state may make certain requirements that seem to it desirable or important for the proper education of those future citizens who go to schools maintained by the states, or whether the pupils in those schools may be relieved from those requirements if they run counter to the consciences of their parents. . . ." (*Id.* at 657) He believed that the state has the "constitutional power to make reasonable provisions for the proper instruction of children in schools maintained by it." (*Id.* at 658)

Apparently the *Barnette* decision has settled the flag salute controversy permanently — at least as far as the courts are concerned. Nevertheless, there are still some diehard school officials who are unwilling to accept the decision as a ruling precedent. Consequently the issue has been adjudicated in state courts several times since *Barnette*. In general, the state courts have followed the legal precedent established in the last previous United States Supreme Court ruling.

For example, in a 1966 case (*Holden* v. *Board of Education of the City of Elizabeth*, 46 N.J. 281, 216 A.2d 387, 1966) the Supreme Court of New Jersey upheld the action of the Commissioner of Education who ordered a school board to reinstate children who had been excluded from school because of their refusal to salute the flag of the United States. Their refusal was based upon their religion (Islam) which "taught that their sole allegiance was to Almighty God Allah and that the flag was but a symbol, it would be contrary to their teachings to pledge allegiance to any flag." (*Id.* at 388)

The statutes of New Jersey require the pupils in each school to salute and pledge allegiance to the flag every school day — except "children who have conscientious scruples against such pledge or salute." (*Id.* at 389)

The court expressed regret that the Islam teachings were

> such as to cause children not to participate in a common ceremony of respect to the flag, which is itself the emblem of those freedoms which all Americans are privileged to enjoy. However, he is cognizant of the fact that those freedoms, as contemplated by Federal and State Constitutions and by State law, are broad enough to encompass the beliefs of those who, like the petitioners, claim conscientious scruples. (*Id.* at 391)

§ 3.5. Compelling participation in religious exercises.

Very few curriculum issues, if any, concerning disputes between parents and schools have been litigated more often than that of pupil participation in religious exercises. Required reading of passages from the Bible and recitation of prayers have been the most vigorously disputed and litigated of the various religious exercises.

Although dozens of court decisions have been rendered on the legality of religious exercises in the public school curriculum, reference need not be made here to more than those which have reached the United States Supreme Court. After all, a decision of the highest court in the land is final and supersedes all those of lower-level courts.

Bible reading. — A prominent court case (*Doremus* v. *Board of Education,* 5 N.J. 435, 75 A.2d 880, 1950) which ultimately went to the United States Supreme Court for final disposal, typifies the early stage of judicial reaction to litigation regarding the legality of required Bible reading in the public schools. The case arose in New Jersey in 1950. Here, certain parents brought action against the school board and the state to test the constitutionality of a statute which provided that "at least five verses taken from that portion of the Holy Bible known as the Old Testament shall be read, or caused to be read, without comment, in each public school classroom."

In challenging the constitutionality of the statute the appellants in the case presented the following line of reasoning:

The principle of the separation of the church and the state is established in the constitution of the United States, namely the first and fourteenth amendments which prohibit the intermingling of religious and secular education in the public schools; the reading of the Bible and the reciting of the Lord's Prayer in the public schools are religious services, religious exercises and religious instruction; they are themselves in aid of one or more religions in preference of one religion or another; and therefore those acts are contrary to the named constitutional provisions. (*Id.* at 881)

The Supreme Court of New Jersey disagreed with the above allegations. It not only upheld the constitutionality of the disputed statutes but commented on its appropriateness and timeliness in the following words:

While it is necessary that there be a separation between church and state, it is not necessary that the state should be stripped of religious sentiment. It may be a tragic experience for this country and for its conception of life, liberty and the pursuit of happiness if our people lose their religious feeling and are left to live their lives without faith. . . . We are at a crucial hour in which it may behoove our people to conserve all of the elements which have made our land what it is. Faced with this threat to the continuance of elements deeply imbedded in our national life the adoption of a public policy with respect thereto is a reasonable function to be performed by those on whom responsibility lies. (*Id.* at 888)

The case was appealed to the United States Supreme Court where, in a six to three decision, it was dismissed for want of jurisdiction, thus affirming the decision of the state court. (*Doremus* v. *Board of Education*, 342 U.S. 429, 1952)

In 1963, another Bible reading case (*Abington School District* v. *Schempp*, 374 U.S. 203, 1963) developed which was to be met head-on by the United States Supreme Court. In contrast to the *Doremus* case, this case was to be decided upon the merits, rather than upon jurisdictional technicalities.

Here a challenged Pennsylvania law originally stipulated that: "At least ten verses from the Holy Bible shall be read without comment, at the opening of each public school on each school day, by the teacher in charge...."

The Schempp family — husband, wife and three children — all of whom were of the Unitarian faith, brought suit to enjoin enforcement of the statute because specific doctrines purveyed by a literal reading of the Bible "were contrary to the religious beliefs which they held and to their familial teaching."

After the district court had ruled against the statute, another sentence was added before it went to the Supreme Court for a ruling: "Any child shall be excused from such Bible reading upon written request of his parents or his guardian." Addition of the exemption clause, however, failed to deter the Court from declaring the law unconstitutional, as is evidenced by the court's statement:

> The fact that some pupils, or theoretically all pupils, might be excused from attendance does not mitigate the obligatory nature of the ceremony.

. . . Since the statute requires the reading of the "Holy Bible," a Christian document, the practice . . . prefers the Christian religion. (*Id.* at 210-11)

Justice Clark, who wrote the majority opinion made a statement that since has been quoted many times:

> It is no defense to urge that the religious practices here may be relatively minor encroachments on the First Amendment. The breach of neutrality that is today a trickling stream may all too soon become a raging torrent and, in the words of Madison, "it is proper to take alarm at the first experiment on our liberties." (*Id.* at 225)

In conclusion the court remarked:

> The place of religion in our society is an exalted one, achieved through a long tradition of reliance on the home, the church and the inviolable citadel of the individual heart and mind. We have come to recognize through bitter experience that it is not within the power of government to invade that citadel, whether the purpose or effect be to aid or oppose, to advance or retard. In the relationship between man and religion, the State is firmly committed to a position of neutrality. Though the application of the rule itself is clearly and concisely stated in the words of the First Amendment. (*Id.* at 226)

Recitation of prayers. — A widely publicized case (*Engle* v. *Vitale*, 370 U.S. 421, 1962) on the legality of mandated prayers in the public school was adjudicated by the United States Supreme Court in 1962 — just one year prior to the *Schempp* decision. In the minds of many legal experts the decision in this case presaged other decisions to follow with respect to inclusion of all religious exercises in the public school curriculum.

This case originated in New York after the State Board of Regents composed the following brief prayer which they recommended for the public schools of New York: "Almighty God, we acknowledge our dependence upon thee, and we beg Thy blessings upon us, our parents, our teachers and our Country."

Shortly after the practice of reciting the Regents' prayer was adopted by the school district of New Hyde Park, the parents of ten pupils brought action in a New York State court, insisting that "use of this official prayer in the public schools was contrary to the beliefs, religions, or religious practices of both themselves and their children." (*Id.* at 423)

The parents further contended that the district's regulation ordering the recitation of this particular prayer was a violation of the First Amendment of the federal Constitution which was made applicable to the State of New York by the Fourteenth Amendment of said Constitution.

The practice of reciting the Regents' prayer as required by the school district was held legal by the Court of Appeals, whereupon it was appealed to the United States Supreme Court. In a six to one decision (Justices Frankfurter and White took no part in the decision of this case) it was finally ruled that the required recitation of this particular prayer was unconstitutional. Justice Black, writing for the majority, noted that since all parties in the case agreed that the prayer was religious in nature, its use in the public schools was a practice wholly inconsistent with the Establishment Clause of the First Amendment to the Constitution. The court reasoned that: "in this country it is no part of the business of government to compose official prayers for any group of the American people to recite as a part of a religious program carried on by the government." (*Id.* at 425)

Justice Stewart, the lone dissenter in the case, did not believe the State of New York had violated the Constitution but rather what it had done was

> to recognize and to follow the deeply entrenched and highly cherished spiritual traditions of our Nation — traditions which come down to us from those who almost two hundred years ago avowed their "firm Reliance on the Protection of divine Providence" when they proclaimed the freedom and independence of this brave new world. (*Id.* at 450)

Despite the United States Supreme Court's decision in the *Engle* case in 1962, the issue of reciting prayers in public schools did not come to rest. Another such case (*De Spain* v. *De Kalb Community School District* (Ill.), 384 F.2d 836, 1968) reached the United States Court of Appeals, Seventh Circuit, in 1968. Here the higher court reversed a federal district court's ruling which had upheld the recitation of a verse (prayer) by children in a kindergarten class before their morning snack. The verse read:

> We thank you for the flowers so sweet;
> We thank you for the food we eat;
> We thank you for the birds that sing;
> We thank you for everything.

In the original text, the last line of the verse read: "We thank you, God, for everything." In an attempt to mollify those who alleged that the verse was actually a prayer and that the recitation constituted a religious exercise, the word "God" was deleted. The deletion, however, did not mitigate the objections of the plaintiffs. Neither did it alter the opinion of the Court of Appeals as is indicated by the Court's comment:

> We are of the view that the verse is a prayer and that its compulsory recitation by kindergarten students in a public school comes within the proscription of the first amendment, as interpreted by the Supreme Court in the "school prayers" cases. (*Id.* at 837)

The court's strict interpretation of the Establishment Clause of the First Amendment is evidenced by the following statement:

> It is not to be gainsaid that the verse may have commendable virtues in teaching kindergarten children "good manners" and "gratitude," to use Mrs. Watne's [the teacher's] words. The fact, however, that children through the use of required schoolroom prayers are likely to become more grateful for the things they receive or that they may become better citizens does not justify the use of compulsory prayer in our public school systems. As the plaintiffs point out, if prayers which tend to teach and inculcate these virtues are not within the ambit of the bar imposed by the first amendment against such religious activity, any religious activity of whatever nature could be justified by public officials on the basis that the activity has beneficial secular purposes; as a result the Supreme Court's admonition in *Engle* and *Schempp* would become meaningless. (*Id.* at 839)

§ 3.6. Barring married students from non-classroom activities.

Cases discussed in this section differ from those already referred to in that they do not specifically involve parents; they do, however, involve married students who eventually may become parents. Most married students are concerned with the curriculum offerings made available to them — both in the classroom and outside the classroom.

The concern of school officials over student marriages is reflected in the numerous policies formulated to regulate school activities of married students as a means of curbing high-school marriages. Some of the board regulations have been so controversial and objectionable as to trigger litigation. At least a dozen cases involving regulations of married students have reached courts of record. The most recent — and applicable to this report — are those pertaining to restrictions of school activities afforded to married students, such as those carried on outside the classroom and usually referred to as "extracurricular activities" — particularly athletic.

The first applicable case (*Kissick* v. *Garland Independent School District* (Tex.), 330 S.W.2d 708, 1959) received nation-wide attention by students of school law. The case report reveals that *Kissick*, a football player, sought to restrain enforcement of a board resolution which provided that "married students be restricted wholly to classroom work and that they be barred from participating in athletics." Among the contentions made by *Kissick* were that (1) the resolution in question was arbitrary, capricious, discriminatory and unreasonable, and (2) it was violative of public policy in that it penalized marriage.

It was "admitted that physical education is a required course of the school; the playing of football being sufficient to obtain credit for that compulsory course; also that the resolution was passed, in the main, to discourage juvenile marriages among students. . . ." (*Id.* at 709-10) Nevertheless, the Texas court upheld the board regulation. Apparently it placed considerable weight upon the findings of a PTA study indicating "ill effects of married students participating in extra-curricular activities with unmarried students."

The assumption that the *Kissick* case established a precedent that would be followed in other jurisdictions was almost disproved by a Michigan case (*Cochrane* v. *Board of Education*, 360 Mich. 390, 103 N.W.2d 569, 1960) which involved two boys who married several weeks before the school board adopted a rule that "married students attending school shall not be eligible to participate in any co-curricular activities — such as competitive sports." The two boys, who had previously participated in competitive sports, filed a writ of mandamus to compel the school board to admit them to the co-curricular activities. After a lower court ruled that the board resolution was legal, the case was appealed to the state supreme court, but before it could be tried there, the two boys graduated. This, of course, made the issue "moot." Nevertheless, the higher court rendered an "advisory opinion." The court was evenly divided in reversing and affirming the ruling of the lower court.

Another case (*State* v. *Stevenson*, 27 Ohio Op. 2d 223, 189 N.E.2d 181, 1962), resulted from a board regulation which retroactively prohibited a married boy who was a "star" basketball player from continuing to participate in the school's athletic program. In upholding the board regulation, the court was apparently influenced by a statistical report showing an "alarming" marriage-dropout relationship. The court ignored an opinion of the Attorney General of Ohio who contended that "a board of education may not lawfully adopt a regulation prohibiting married students from participation in extra-curricular activities promoted by the school as a part of the regular school program. He made the observation that extra-curricular activities 'have become an integral part of contemporary education'." (*Id.* at 187)

The fourth case (*Starkey* v. *Board of Education*, 14 Utah 2d 227, 381 P.2d 718, 1963) reaching a state supreme court arose in Utah in 1963. The factors involved in the case were quite similar to those of the three preceding cases reported. The court's ruling was also similar to those in other jurisdictions in that the board's regulation prohibiting a married boy from participating in the athletic program was legal. As did the other courts, the Utah Supreme Court placed emphasis upon the fact that school boards, and not the courts, are endowed with the power to regulate the schools. Judicial interference would be justified only with evidence of the board's abuse of discretionary authority.

As in the preceding case reported, the court was not influenced by plaintiff's contention that "the requirement to maintain a uniform system of public schools, which shall be open to all children of the State . . . must include the extra-curricular activities and not merely the academic pursuits since the latter made up only a part of the total school program." (*Id.* at 720)

At the time of this writing the last case (*Board of Directors of Independent School District of Waterloo* v. *Green*, 259 Ia. 1260, 147 N.W.2d 854, 1967) dealing with the issue was adjudicated by the Supreme Court of Iowa in 1967. Here the board of education adopted a policy barring married students from participation in extracurricular activities. A high-school boy who was a regular player on the basketball team married just before his senior year. In accordance with the board policy he was denied the right to play on the team. He sought and obtained an injunction from the District Court preventing enforcement of the rule. The board, in collaboration with the Iowa Association of School Boards, appealed to the Supreme Court which reversed the decision of the District Court, thereby upholding the board rule.

It would appear from the concluding statement of the Supreme Court that the issue was settled with unanimity and finality:

> We conclude the rule adopted by defendant board barring married students from participating in extra-curricular activities is neither arbitrary, unreasonable, irrational, unauthorized, nor unconstitutional. In taking this position we do not stand alone. (*Id.* at 860)

It is significant to note, however, that three of the justices dissented.

Chapter 4

CONTROL OVER STUDENT BEHAVIOR

§ 4.0. Generally.

Court cases referred to in Chapter 2 indicate that children, within specified age limits, may be compelled to attend a school. Even though legislators and school officials must take into account the natural rights of parents in the matter of compulsory school attendance, the important fact is that children may be compelled to attend some kind of an approved school — public, private or home.

Also the court cases presented in Chapter 3 reveal that pupils may be required to pursue certain studies and activities offered in the school curriculum. Here again legislators and school officials do not possess unlimited authority in determining precisely the activities in which the pupils may or may not participate; the parent possesses certain natural rights here too which must be respected. Nevertheless, within statutory and constitutional limitations, a curriculum must be provided, the offerings of which may be prescribed or restricted.

Even though school attendance and curricula are essential, certain other conditions are necessary before a complete educational opportunity is possible. The school must be conducted in an orderly fashion. Rules of conduct are necessary to provide an environment conducive to the educational process. Therefore the statutes of many states confer on boards of education the power to make and enforce rules governing the conduct of pupils. Even without the statutory provisions, school boards have the inherent power to make rules and regulations for the discipline, government and management of the schools and the pupils who attend them.

This power to make rules and regulations for governing pupil conduct descends in some degree to the administrative and teaching staffs. Within the general policies formulated by the board, the administrative and teaching personnel are permitted and required to make the necessary rules to maintain order in and out of the classroom. The general legal view is that school administrators and teachers may prescribe reasonable rules and regulations which are pertinent and commensurate to their sphere of responsibility.

Frequently rules and regulations for student behavior — whether decreed by legislatures, school boards or school personnel are objectionable to certain students and their parents, and challenged with respect to their legality. Ultimately, then, the courts may be called upon to determine the legality of the schools' contested rules and regulations which are presumably designed to promote such discipline, decorum and morale as are conceived by school authorities to be necessary for educational purposes. Usually the courts will refuse to interfere with the discretionary authority of school officials in matters of school discipline. Only when the rules and regulations are judged to be unreasonable, arbitrary or unconstitutional are the courts likely to intercede.

After rules governing discipline have been adopted by the school board or prescribed by statute, the administrative and instructional staff of the school should be responsible for their implementation, or, in cases of deficiency, to even supplement them with their own rules and regulations. Obviously in order to maintain proper order in the classroom, the teacher must be granted some discretionary authority for correctiveness to meet possible exigencies.

Even though parents, as the natural guardians of their children, have the right to and responsibility for the custody, care and education of their minor children, their parental authority is temporarily superseded by that of school authorities during school hours. The legal principle has been generally accepted that during school hours, the teacher stands *in loco parentis* (in place of the parent) for purposes of maintaining discipline. During recent years, however, the *in loco parentis* concept appears to be losing its stability. Although it is still generally considered applicable and appropriate at the elementary level, at the college level it has virtually been abandoned, and is waning at the high school level.

A review of all court cases, in recent years, concerning the control of student behavior, reveals an increasing rate of cases at the secondary level as compared with those at the elementary level. Most of those referred to in this investigation deal with alleged disruptive behavior of high school students. A fair sampling of cases involves the "freedom of expressions" and "due process" provisions of the First and Fourteenth Amendments of the United States Constitution.

§ 4.1. Regulating student appearance.

Wearing of hair styles by boys. — Extreme hair styles worn by high-school students exemplify a means of expressing opposition to "the establishment." Students and parents may claim that a school board policy regulating the style of a boy's hair is an invasion of family authority over the student. School board regulations of hair styles became an issue to be disputed in local communities and litigated at the lower court level in the early 1960's. Not until 1965, however, was the issue adjudicated in a court of record.

The pertinent facts of the first state supreme court case (*Leonard* v. *School Committee of Attleboro*, 349 Mass. 704, 212 N.E.2d 468, 1965) concerning the issue reveal that (1) the principal of a high school suspended a seventeen-year-old boy who refused to cut his long hair which he claimed was essential for his image as a musician; (2) the school board upheld the principal's action as a necessity for maintaining proper school decorum; (3) the parents of the boy brought suit seeking the boy's return to school (with long hair intact) and finally (4) the Massachusetts Supreme Court agreed with the school authorities that the boy's hair, grown well over his ears "could disrupt and impede school decorum," and therefore ruled that school officials had the right to order him to get a normal haircut.

Plaintiff parents had contended that a "regulation which bars a student from attending classes solely because of length or appearance of hair is unreasonable and arbitrary, since these matters are in no way connected with the successful operation of a public school." They further contended that "the challenged ruling is an invasion of family privacy touching matters occurring while he is at home and within the exclusive control of the parents." (*Id.* at 472-73)

The court refused to pass upon the wisdom or desirability of the school regulation, but nevertheless responded to the parents contentions by stating:

> So here, the domain of family privacy must give way in so far as a regulation reasonably calculated to maintain school discipline may affect it. The rights of other students, and the interest of teachers, administrators and the community at large in a well run and efficient school system are paramount. . . . It may be conceded that the length and appearance of the plaintiff's hair are essential to his image as a performer, and hence to his ability to follow his chosen profession. But the discretionary powers of the committee are broad, and

the courts will not reverse its decision unless it can be shown it acted arbitrarily or capriciously. *(Id.* at 473)

Just one year after the *Leonard* case, a Texas case (*Ferrell* v. *Dallas Independent School District* (Tex.), 261 F. Supp. 545, 1966) on the issue of regulating hair styles of high school students came before a federal court. In many respects it was similar to the preceding case. It involved four high school students who were members of a musical group known as "Sounds Unlimited." The boys comprising the group were denied admission to the public schools, because of their extreme hair styles — as judged by the school principal. The ruling of the United States District Court was similar to that of the Massachusetts Supreme Court in that it upheld the action of the school authorities.

Although much of the testimony in the case appeared to be somewhat ludicrous, the court gave it serious consideration because it had created a great deal of publicity and aroused a great deal of feeling in the community. The court's reasoning for its decision is portrayed in its concluding comment:

> Plaintiffs contend naturally that their primary interest is to get an education, but it appears that they want their education on their own terms. It is inconceivable that a school administrator could operate his school successfully if required by the courts to follow the dictates of the students as to what their appearance shall be, what they shall wear, what hours they will attend, etc. . . . One of the most important aims of the school should be to educate the individual to live successfully with other people in our democracy. Since the school

authorities, by legislative grant, control the public educational system, their regulations play a part in the educational process. . . . It does not appear from the facts of their particular case that there has been any abuse of discretion on the part of the school authorities. On the contrary, it appears that they acted reasonably under the circumstances, taking into consideration those individual students *and* the need for an academic atmosphere. (*Id.* at 552)

Three years later a student in California was suspended from school for alleged violation of a school policy which prohibited "extremes" of hair styles. The resulting case (*Myers* v. *Arcata Union High School District*, 75 Cal. Rptr. 68, 1969) is significant in that its ruling is in contrast with those of the two preceding cases referred to.

After suspension from school for not abiding by a school policy regarding personal appearance, a minor student brought action in mandamus, through his mother as "guardian ad litem," and against the school authorities to compel his reinstatement.

The student and his mother argued that the school policy which states "extremes of hair styles are not acceptable," was not violated. Their main point of contention was that the policy was so vaguely stated that compliance would be uncertain. The trial court agreed that the term "extreme" had no specific meaning.

During interrogations at the hearing, witnesses expressed personal opinions as to what constituted an "extreme" hair style. According to the vice-principal's standards of a male hair style, the hair is too long when "it obscures the student's ears, or reaches his collar or is starting to turn up." Nothing that definitive was stated in the policy. Moreover, neither the student nor his mother "was told how much of a haircut would produce a style which was 'acceptable' or something other than 'extreme.' " (*Id.* at 71)

In its ruling the court declared:

> The words "extremes of hair styles" convey no commonly understood meaning, and whether one such style as Arcata High School was "extreme" was neither determinable nor predictable by anyone except the vice-principal. (*Id.* at 75)

In justifying its ruling which differed with those of preceding cases on the same issue the court stated:

> We recognize that school regulations not unlike the one here involved were upheld in each of the two principal cases which deal with male high school students who were suspended because of their hair. . . . We do not read either decision as constitutional authority for the enforceability of a "policy" which proscribes — but which does not define — "extremes of hair styles." (*Id.* at 75)

Therefore the Appellate Court affirmed the trial court's decision issuing a writ of mandate to compel reinstatement of the plaintiff in the school.

Vagueness is not the only reason for which a school board policy prohibiting the wearing of long hair may be declared unconstitutional. For example, as shown in a federal case (*Breen* v. *Kahl* (Wis.), 296 F. Supp. 702, 1969) a board policy was found to be illegal even though the regulation of the Williams Bay Board was specific: "Hair should be washed, combed and worn so it does not hang below the collar line in the back, over the ears on the side and must be above the eyebrows. Boys should be clean shaven; long sideburns are out." (*Id.* at 703)

Thomas Breen and another boy refused to comply with the haircut regulation and were accordingly expelled from school on the grounds that their refusal "constituted a disruptive influence or factor within the school." Plaintiff Breen, through his mother, challenged the constitutionality of the regulation and denied that the long hair caused a disruption in the school.

After reviewing the facts of the case, Judge Doyle made the following statement:

> The record contains no suggestion that the length of the hair constituted a health problem or a physical obstruction or danger to any person; I find that it did not. At no time while either plaintiff was in attendance in the high school with hair longer than the Board standard was any disruption or disturbance caused by the length of his hair. (*Id.* at p. 704)

The judge expressed the opinion that wearing one's hair at a certain length "is a form of constitutionally protected expression . . . that the manner in which many younger people now wear their hair is an expression of cultural revolt." (*Id.* at 705)

Judge Doyle emphasized "that when a school board undertakes to expel a public school student, it is undertaking to apply the terrible organized force of the state, just as surely as it is applied by the police, the courts, the prison warden, or the militia." (*Id.* at 707)

For these reasons and others given in the opinion the judge "adjudged that the regulation of the Williams Bay Board of Education limiting the length of male students' hair, requiring male students to be clean shaven, and prohibiting sideburns, violate the due process clause of the Constitution of the United States, and is null and void." (*Id.* at 709-10)

In another hairstyle case (*Griffin* v. *Tatum* (Ala.), 300 F. Supp. 60, 1969), a United States District Court had to decide whether a school board regulation was constitutional which, in part, required "that the hairline in back must be shingled or tapered as opposed to being blocked and must be well above the collar." (*Id.* at 61)

A high school boy who was suspended for failure to comply with this regulation brought action, with his father, against the school authorities so as to be readmitted to the school without further disciplinary action.

In defending their action the school authorities offered the following reasons as justification for the regulation and the suspension:

> ... boys' haircuts that do not conform to the regulation cause the boys to comb their hair in classes and to pass combs, both of which are distracting; cause the boys to be late for classes because they linger in the restrooms combing their hair; cause the boys to congregate at a mirror provided for girls to use while combing their hair; in some instances, cause an unpleasant odor, as hair of a length in excess of that provided by the regulation often results in the hair being unclean; cause some of the boys who do not conform to the haircut regu-

lation to be reluctant about engaging in physical education activities (presumably because they do not want to "muss" their hair) ; and, finally cause resentment on the part of other students who do not like haircuts that do not conform to the school's haircut regulation. (*Id.* at 61)

Not being convinced by this argument, the court ruled that the board regulation was unconstitutional and accordingly ordered that the plaintiff student be readmitted and that all evidence of his suspension be expunged from the school record. In support of its ruling the court declared:

> The school authorities' "justification" or the reasons they advance for the necessity for such a haircut rule, completely fail. If combing hair or passing combs in classes is distracting, the teachers, in the exercise of their authority, may stop this without requiring that the head be shorn. If there is congestion at the girls' mirrors, or if the boys are late for classes because they linger in the restrooms grooming their hair, appropriate disciplinary measures may be taken to stop this without requiring a particular hair style. . . . As to the fear that some students might take action against the students who wear hair longer than the regulation now permits, suffice it to say that the exercise of a constitutional right cannot be curtailed because of an undifferentiated fear that the exercise of that right will produce a violent reaction on the part of those who would deprive one of the exercise of that constitutional right. (*Id.* at 63)

> In short, the freedom here protected is the right to some breathing space for the individual into which the government may not intrude without

carrying a substantial burden of justification. (*Id.* at 62)

After several consecutive federal court decisions, which voided school board regulations of hairstyles, it appeared that the rulings had settled the issue permanently. Nevertheless, in 1969 a contrasting decision was rendered.

In the instant case (*Crews* v. *Cloncs* (Ind.), 303 F. Supp. 1370, 1969), a 16-year-old boy brought action, by his father, against school officials, and requested injunctive relief requiring the defendant school authorities to admit him to school without his first complying with the school's requirement of a satisfactory hair length and style. In brief, the requirement stipulated that hair length shall be "above the collar, above the ears and out of the eyes."

It was noted that prior to the suspension, "the plaintiff's hair was parted in the middle and hung several inches below the shoulders in back and on chest in front, in what would normally be described as feminine in style." (*Id.* at 1372)

That the Court was aware of the extremely changing styles of youth, in accordance with the times, is evidenced by its statement: "The long hair case of today may be a shaven head case tomorrow, or a brilliantly dyed hair case of some other time. The possible extremes of dress and attire are nearly unlimited." It added "this Court has no desire to interfere with the duly constituted authority of school boards and school administrators to adopt and to enforce reasonable rules and regulations. Neither does the Court propose to substitute its judgment for that of school boards and administrators absent a clearly defined violation of Constitutional rights." (*Id.* at 1374)

The Court made some reconciliatory reference to the decision of this case because of its difference with that in *Breen* v. *Kahl:*

> It is important to note that the disruption found here resulted not from the very fact that a student had violated a rule; rather, it resulted directly from plaintiff's wearing long hair. Had disruption resulted indirectly merely because a pupil chose to flaunt the school's authority by violating a rule, it would lend absolutely no constitutional support to the rule itself. (*Id.* at 1376)

The Court was convinced that the plaintiff was given constitutionally valid consideration, which complied with *procedural due process rights* under the Fourteenth Amendment. Moreover, it found that there was no unconstitutional infringement on the plaintiff's *substantive due process rights* under the First and Fourteenth Amendments. The Court concluded, therefore, that "the plaintiff is not entitled to an injunction requiring defendants to admit him to North Central High School without first complying with the school's regulations as to length of hair." (*Id.* at 1377)

The decision, *for* the school board's regulation, in *Crews* v. *Cloncs,* however, did not reverse a trend; almost simultaneously, another federal court ruled against a school official's regulation of hairstyles. The Court's decision in this case (*Richards* v. *Thurston* (Mass.), 304 F. Supp. 449, 1969), is significant in that

(1) it was in contrast with the decision in *Leonard* v. *School Committee of Attleboro*, also in Massachusetts, in 1965; (2) it was stated in most emphatic terms; and (3) it summarized the rulings of the several preceding federal court cases on the issue.

In this case a 17-year-old boy, by his father, filed a complaint against a school principal and sought restoration to his status as a member of the senior class after having been suspended for refusal to have his hair cut in conformance to standards of the principal. The Court found no reason for the principal's official act except possibly "the principal's personal prejudice, the community conventions of the first half of the Twentieth Century, and the views of some contemporaries. . . ." (*Id.* at 451) Moreover, no claim was made that plaintiff's hairstyle involved health or sanitary risks to him or to others, or that it would interfere with his performance in school work, or create disciplinary problems.

The Court indicated its cognizance of altering hairstyles from time to time throughout the ages by making references to the unusual styles of such prominent individuals as Sampson, President Lincoln, and Chief Justice Hughes. Then further justification for permitting hair to grow longer than was previously the custom, was suggested by the Court as follows:

> Today many of both the younger and the older generations have avoided the increased cost of barbering by allowing their locks or burnsides to grow to greater length than when a haircut cost a quarter of a dollar. (*Id.* at 451)

After considerable dicta, by way of emphasizing the rationale for its decision, the Court concluded by ordering that:

> Plaintiff is entitled to a decree (1) that he be reinstated forthwith as a student in good standing in the Marlboro High School with the same rights, privileges, and immunities as those he had before his suspension, (2) that there be expunged from that school's records any notation of the suspension against which he complained and of the absences due thereto, (3) that defendant be enjoined from suspending or disciplining him on account of his hairstyle, and (4) that plaintiff recover his costs. (*Id.* at 453)

Wearing of beard by boys. — The wearing of a beard has also been a cause for litigation. In the only such case (*Akin* v. *Board of Education of Riverside Unified School District*, 68 Cal. Rptr. 557, 1968) reported by a court of record, a fifteen-year-old minor was refused admission to the Polytechnic High School in Riverside, California, because he had a beard — even though the beard was neat in appearance and trimmed regularly.

The involved minor, acting through his mother as "guardian ad litem," filed a petition for writ of mandate to allow him to enroll at Polytechnic High School without having to shave off his beard in conformity with the "Good Grooming Policy" of the school board. The Superior Court denied the writ and appeal was taken.

Testimony revealed that "the boy was a good student and well-behaved; his relationship with the other students was satisfactory; the beard caused no distraction to other students after the initial reaction diminished. ..." (*Id.* at 559)

Petitioners contended the requirement was in violation of the First Amendment as ruled in a former case (see *Finot* v. *Pasadena City Board of Education,* 58 Cal. Rptr. 520, 1967) where "a teacher's right to wear a beard was viewed as a protected personal liberty granted him under the 'due process' provisions of the federal constitution, and further as a form of expression entitled to the 'peripheral protection' of the First Amendment." (*Id.* at 560)

To this contention the court replied:

> While a male adult teacher may enjoy a constitutional right to wear a beard where good cause for a school's administrative policy banning the wearing of beards by teachers has not been shown to exist, and assuming that such a constitutional right vests by implication in a minor student, it is manifestly clear that not every public restriction or limitation placed upon the exercise of secondary students' constitutional rights is *ipso facto* prohibited. (*Id.* at 560)

Apparently the court relied upon the professional judgment of the school administrators in determining the effects of a bearded student on other students as is indicated by the following comment:

> The administrative policy of the school board was the result of the considered judgment of a number of persons who were experienced in the field of education; it was the opinion of administrative and teaching experts that the wearing of a beard would be definitely disruptive of the edu-

cational process; such a disturbance would have a prejudicial effect on the educational environment and adverse effects on other students; the academic system and maintenance of discipline were best served when there were no such influences; proper classroom atmosphere and decorum flourished where such influences were not present and where students were not subjected to distraction by other pupils. (*Id.* at 562)

Consequently, the Court of Appeals ruled that "the trial court was justified in concluding that the regulation subjected to attack herein contributed to the maintenance of order and decorum within the education system." (*Id.* at 563)

Wearing of slacks by girls. — Protests against school regulations of girls' clothing are usually resolved before reaching a court of record. A case (*Scott* v. *Board of Education, Union Free School District #17, Hicksville*, 305 N.Y.S.2d 601, 1969), however, did reach a New York Supreme Court where the question was posed as to whether a school board has the power to proscribe the wearing of slacks in school by female students.

Among the facts of the case it was revealed that the dress regulation adopted by the Hicksville High School prohibited "girls from wearing slacks except when permitted by principal upon petition by student council when warranted by cold weather." A tenth-grade student, whose family did not have the financial means to buy clothing which conformed to the dress code, wore slacks to school without permission of the principal. Because of her violation of the dress code she was placed in detention, thereby missing her classes. Consequently the girl and her parents brought action to nullify the school dress code.

Although the Court found nothing in the Education Law which dealt explicitly with dress, it did note that the Board had "implied power to regulate dress for reasons of safety, in addition to the express power to do so for reasons of order and discipline."

The Court contended, however, that since the Board's action bore "no reasonable relation to safety, order or discipline," the Board had acted "beyond its authority." To justify its ruling, the Court concluded as follows:

> Does the proscription of slacks for female students fall within the perimeters of the Board's authority? The simple facts that it applies only to female students makes no differentiation as to the kind of slacks mandates a negative answer, for those facts make evident that what is being enforced is style or taste and not safety, order or discipline. A regulation against the wearing of bell-bottomed slacks by students, male or female, who ride bicycles to school can probably be justified in the interest of safety, as can, in the interest of discipline, a regulation against slacks that are so skintight and, therefore, revealing as to provoke or distract students of the opposite sex, and, in the interest of order, a regulation against slacks to the bottoms of which small bells have been attached. Such regulations are valid because they relate the prohibition to an area within the Board's authorized concerns; the flat prohibition of all slacks is invalid precisely because it does not. (*Id.* at 606)

The application of "due process" rights of students in issues of school board regulations pertaining to student appearance and similar matters is receiving judicial scrutinization. A Florida case (*Conyers et al. v. Pinellas County Board of Public Instruction*, Circuit Court for Pinellas County, Circuit Civil No. 16,634, 1969) which was adjudicated at the beginning of the 1969-70 school year is in point. Although the case has not yet reached a higher state or federal court it is referred to here because of its uniqueness and significance.

In this case two boys, joined by their parents, requested and were granted a temporary injunction forbidding the Clearwater High School from enforcing a regulation on haircuts. The pertinent issue raised by the complaint was "whether the public schools must accord due process of law — charges, notice of hearing, time to prepare for hearing, confrontation of witnesses, appeal, stay pending appeal — in enforcing the school regulations respecting hair length." (*Id.* at 1) The reaction of Judge Holley, who rendered the opinion, is indicated in his following emphatic comments:

> If parents cannot be required to provide procedural due process of law with respect to parental authority, can due process be required of the public school system standing in loco parentis? ...
>
> There is no doubt whatever in my mind that there is no right of procedural due process with respect to the disciplining of a child by a parent. There is no doubt whatever in my mind of the right of the parent to delegate this parental authority

to another without the creation of any right of procedural due process in the child. Does the constitutional delegation of this authority by the citizens without the specific consent of the parent give rise to the right to procedural due process where the specific consent to the delegation would not? It is my opinion that no right to procedural due process arises by such governmental delegation, and this order is predicted primarily on this conclusion. (*Id.* at 6)

In his concluding dicta, Judge Holley points out the difficulties which would be encountered by school officials if pupils were granted procedural due process in all matters of school discipline:

Consider the chaos in our public schools if we are to permit seven-year olds and eleven-year olds and fifteen-year olds and seventeen-year olds to demand notice, time to prepare for hearing, confrontation of witnesses, stay of judgment, and appeal each time a school official charges one with violation of a valid regulation and proposed appropriate disciplinary action. In this respect there can be no logical distinction between a fifteen-year old who wants to wear his hair long and the seven-year old who does not want to wear a shirt.

Our public school authorities have had wished upon them much more than they have asked. This court will not impose upon them the impossible. (*Id.* at 8)

§ 4.2. Prohibiting display of insignia as a protest gesture.

Wearing armbands. — Another method of expressing opposition to certain governmental activities is the wearing of symbolic insignia by students. The advantage of this technique over the wearing of long hair or beards is that it is subject to quick adaptation. An applicable court case (*Tinker* v. *Des Moines Independent Community School District* (Iowa), 89 S. Ct. 733, 1969) which received nation-wide publicity, had its beginning in 1965 when a group of adults and students in Des Moines met and decided to publicize their objections to the hostilities in Vietnam and their support for a truce by wearing black armbands.

After the school principals became aware of the plan "they met and adopted a policy that any student wearing an armband to school would be asked to remove it, and if he refused he would be suspended until he returned without the armband." (*Id.* at 735)

Three of the Tinker children returned to school with the armbands intact, and were accordingly suspended. Complaint was then filed in a United States District Court, through their father, praying for an injunction restraining the school official from disciplining the offending pupils. "The District Court concluded that the action of the school authorities was reasonable because it was based upon their fear of a disturbance from wearing the armbands." (*Id.* at 737) That decision, however, was reversed by the United States Supreme Court in 1969.

The Supreme Court upheld the pupils' symbolic expression by application of the Free Speech Clause of the First Amendment and stated:

... the wearing of armbands in the circumstances of this case was entirely divorced from actually or potentially disruptive conduct by those participating in it. It was closely akin to "pure speech" which, we have repeatedly held, is entitled to comprehensive protection under the First Amendment. (*Id.* at 736)

The court added that:

> Clearly the prohibition of expression of one particular opinion, at least without evidence that it is necessary to avoid material and substantial interference with school work or discipline, is not constitutionally permissible. . . . In our system, students may not be regarded as closed-circuit recipients of only that which the State chooses to communicate. They may not be confined to the expression of those sentiments that are officially approved. In the absence of a specific showing of constitutionally valid reasons to regulate their speech, students are entitled to freedom of expression of their views. (*Id.* at 739)

Excerpts from the lengthy dissent of Justice Black indicate his apprehensive view of the majority opinion:

> School discipline, like parental discipline, is an integral and important part of training our children to be good citizens. . . . One does not need to be a prophet or the son of a prophet to know that after the Court's holding today that some students in Iowa schools and indeed in all schools will be ready, able, and willing to defy their teachers on practically all orders. This is more unfortunate for the schools since groups of students all over the land are already running loose, conducting break-ins, sit-ins, lie-ins, and smash-ins. . . . I wish, therefore, wholly to disclaim any purpose on my part, to hold that the Federal Constitution compels the teachers, parents and elected school officials to surrender control of the American public

school system to public school students. I dissent.
(*Id.* at 746)

Wearing buttons. — Somewhat comparable to the *Tinker* "armband case," are several "button cases" all of which were adjudicated in federal district courts. The first such case (*Burnside* v. *Byars* (Miss.), 363 F.2d 744, 1966) grew out of a civil rights action for an injunction against high school officials for a regulation prohibiting students from wearing "freedom buttons" with the words, "One Man One Vote," on them.

> The Negro school children who attended an all Negro high school wore the "freedom buttons" as a means of silently communicating an idea and to encourage members of their community to exercise their civil rights. The right to communicate a matter of vital public concern is embraced in the First Amendment right to freedom of speech and therefore is clearly protected against infringement by state officials. (*Id.* at 747)

Apparently the wearing of the buttons caused no commotion in this particular school.

> Even the principal testified that the children were expelled not for causing a commotion or disrupting classes but for violating the school regulations. Thus it appears that the presence of "freedom buttons" did not hamper the school in carrying on its regular schedule of activities; nor would it seem likely that the simple wearing of buttons unaccompanied by improper conduct would ever do so. (*Id.* at 748)

In reversing the decision of the District Court which denied the injunction, the Court of Appeals ruled in favor of the students and declared:

We wish to make it quite clear that we do not applaud any attempt to undermine the authority of the school. We support all efforts made by the school to fashion responsible regulations for the conduct of their students and enforcement of the punishment incurred when such regulations are violated. Obedience to duly constituted authority is a valuable tool, and respect for those in authority must be instilled in our young people.

But with all of this in mind, we must also emphasize that school officials cannot ignore expressions of feelings with which they do not wish to contend. They cannot infringe on their students' right to free and unrestricted expression as guaranteed to them under the First Amendment to the Constitution, where the exercise of such rights in the school buildings and schoolrooms do not materially and substantially interfere with the requirements of appropriate discipline in the operation of the school. (*Id.* at 749)

In a companion case (*Blackwell* v. *Issaquena County Board of Education* (Miss.), 363 F.2d 749, 1966) decided by the same court on the same day, the issue was the same — a civil rights action to enjoin school officials from enforcing a regulation forbidding the wearing of "freedom buttons."

Other pertinent circumstances in this case, however, were markedly different from those in the *Burnside* case. The court explained the differences in the following manner:

In the case now before us, the affidavits and testimony from the District Court present quite a different picture from the record in *Burnside* where no disruption of classes or school routine appeared in the evidence. Here, the District Court was presented with evidence of numerous instances, which have been set out in the statement of facts, where students conducted themselves in a disorderly manner, disrupted classroom procedure, interfered with the proper decorum and discipline of the school and disturbed other students who did not wish to participate in the wearing of the buttons. (*Id.* at 753)

Consequently the Court of Appeals affirmed the decision of the District Court which refused to grant the requested preliminary injunction, and concluded as follows:

The judgment is affirmed but without prejudice to the right of the appellants to relief upon final hearing if the facts justify such relief, emphasizing as we do the importance of the right of freedom of expression and communication as protected by the First Amendment, and the fundamental requirement that school officials should be careful in their monitoring of student expressions in circumstances in which such expression does not substantially interfere with the operation of the school. (*Id.* at 754)

Evidence produced in the *Burnside* case, *supra*, indicated that the wearing of the buttons caused *no* commotion or disorder in the school, but the students who wore the buttons were expelled merely for violating a school regulation; therefore the wearing of the buttons was legally declared permissible. Conversely, in the *Blackwell* case, *supra*, it was evident that the wearing of the buttons *did* disrupt classroom procedure and interfere with the proper decorum and discipline of the school; therefore the school's prohibitive measure was ruled to be legal.

In a later case (*Guzick* v. *Drebus* (Ohio), 305 F. Supp. 472, 1969), a United States District Court ruled that a school board had the right to prohibit the wearing of buttons or other insignia as a *precautionary* measure where there was evidence that to permit such wearing could conceivably cause serious disruption and disorder. In the instant case, the school regulation prohibiting the wearing of insignia as a preventative measure was upheld by the court because of circumstantial evidence which indicated considerable friction between the black students and the white students. The incendiary environment of the school which justified preventative action is evidenced by the following comments:

> Although there have been no crippling disruptions of school activities, Shaw High has a significant, perhaps serious, discipline problem. Students have been threatened in both men's rooms and locker rooms, among other places. These threats have often been accompanied by violence. . . . There have been numerous fights at Shaw, both between blacks and whites and among students of the same race. These fights have occurred both during school hours and in the evening. (*Id.* at 475)

> As the Court has found above, a rule permitting the wearing of some buttons and not others will itself lead to disruptions of the educational process at Shaw. Similarly, the rule which permits the wearing of any button will occasion the wearing of provocative and inciting buttons and will also disrupt the educational process.

The Court finds that the prohibition of buttons and other insignia at Shaw High significantly contributes to the preservation of peace and order, and that the blanket prohibition of buttons and insignia is reasonably related to the prevention of the distractions and disruptive and violent conduct at Shaw High. The Court finds that if all buttons are permitted or if any buttons are permitted, a serious discipline problem will result, racial tensions will be exacerbated, and the educational process will be significantly and substantially disrupted. (*Id.* at 478)

In justifying its decision, which appears to be at variance with decisions of other cases on the same issue, the Court concluded thusly:

The evidence in this case has made it abundantly clear that the school authorities have a factual basis upon which to forecast substantial disruption of, or material interference with, school activities if student behavioral conduct regarding the wearing of buttons is not regulated.

Therefore, the Court finds the issues in this case in favor of the defendants, and the plaintiff's claim for injunctive relief and damages is denied. (*Id.* at 483-84)

§ 4.3. Regulating student demonstrations.

Student demonstrations fall into the same category as riots, boycotts, and sit-ins as a symbol of our times. High school students have observed from college demonstrations the effectiveness of acting in concert to put across an expression of attitude or protest. Because of their immaturity, however, high-school students might not possess the same degree of freedom to demonstrate and to carry on other protest activities as their elders. Nevertheless it is irrefutable that the right of high-school students to demonstrate is protected by the First and Fourteenth Amendments.

As indicated in the cases dealing with the wearing of armbands and buttons, the demonstrations are viewed as a form of expression. If conducted peacefully at the proper times and proper places they are likely to receive judicial sanction — at least at the federal court level. A case (*Edwards* v. *South Carolina*, 372 U.S. 229, 1963) in point arose in South Carolina, where high school students joined college students in attempting to peacefully express their dissatisfaction with allegedly present conditions of discriminatory actions against Negroes.

Circumstances surrounding the case are succinctly stated in certiorari to the Supreme Court of South Carolina as follows:

> Feeling aggrieved by laws of South Carolina which allegedly "prohibited Negro privileges," petitioners, 187 Negro high-school and college students, peacefully assembled at the site of the State Government and there peacefully expressed their grievances "to the citizens of South Carolina, along with the Legislative Bodies of South Carolina." When told by police officials that they must disperse within 15 minutes on pain of arrest, they failed to do so and sang patriotic and religious songs after one of their leaders had delivered a "religious harangue." There was no violence or threat of violence on their part or on the part of any member of the crowd watching them; but petitioners were arrested and convicted of the common-

law crime of breach of the peace, which the State Supreme Court said "is not susceptible of exact definition." (*Id.* at 229)

Although the convictions of the demonstrators were affirmed by the South Carolina Supreme Court, the ruling was reversed by the United States Supreme Court. In support of its action the Court spoke as follows:

> The Fourteenth Amendment does not permit a State to make criminal the peaceful expression of unpopular views. A function of free speech under our system of government is to invite dispute. It may indeed best serve the high purpose when it induces a condition of unrest, creates dissatisfaction with conditions as they are, or even stirs people to anger. Speech is often provocative and challenging. It may strike at prejudice and preconceptions and have profound unsettling effects as it presses for acceptance of an idea. That is why freedom of speech is protected against censorship on punishment, unless shown likely to produce a clear and present danger of a serious substantive evil that arises far above public inconvenience, annoyance, or unrest.... (*Id.* at 237)

Although high-school students may be granted the right to participate in demonstrations, school boards are not free to dismiss students from regularly scheduled classes for that purpose. This is particularly true where planned demonstrations are designed to express views on controversial issues. An illustrative case (*Nistad* v. *Board of Education of City of New York*, 304 N.Y.S.2d 971, 1969) involved a school board's declaration that "teachers and pupils who wish, as a matter of conscience, to participate in planned programs"

— such as demonstrations opposing the Viet Nam War — "outside the schools would be permitted to do so, and the pupils would not be penalized for their absence."

As a consequence of the board's declaration, a junior-high-school student and his mother sought an order directing the school board to rescind its directive and to hold classes as usual on October 15, 1969, which was designated as the day for the demonstrations. They contended that the Board's action "violates their right of freedom of speech under the First and Fourteenth Amendments to the United States Constitution in that it places the affirmative support of government behind a controversial political hypothesis, and that it illegally compels the infant petitioner to profess his views on this conflict." (*Id.* at 973) As indicated by the following statement, the Supreme Court of New York, Richmond County, sanctioned petitioners' contention:

> The issue before this Court is whether or not the Board of Education of the City of New York has the power to act in an area so touching upon matters of opinion and political attitude. The Court thinks it has not. No one takes issue with the fact that the Viet Nam War question comes high in the order of priority, and that it is an emotional and controversial and moral matter. There is no argument with the fact, nor is there an issue before the Court, as to whether or not we are all involved in this. However, the propriety of the issue, emotion, involvement, good intent, etc. cannot be allowed to cause us to turn our backs on our Constitutional heredity and allow the slightest breach of our personal liberties in the name of good intent or honest effort. (*Id.* at 973)

Apparently the Court feared that if the Board's actions were approved:

> Students would quickly get the impression, if they have not already, that they have total freedom, by official edict, to move about and participate in whatever they, in "good conscience," feel right at any time, and absent themselves from school in so doing. An implication might arise, contrary to state law, that attendance in school is secondary to their right to participate in causes morally worthwhile in their minds. (*Id.* at 976)

§ 4.4. Restricting students' freedom of speech and press.

Minor students do not possess unlimited freedom of speech and press. This was revealed in a case (*Scoville* v. *Board of Education of Joliet Township High School District 204* (Ill.), 286 F. Supp. 988, 1968) where students distributed copies of a "literary journal" entitled "Grass High" which contained, in an editorial, derogatory statements about the school administration. For example:

> The editorial went on to criticize school attendance regulations as "utterly idiotic and asinine" and concluded that "Our whole system of education with all its arbitrary rules and schedules seems dedicated to nothing but wasting time." Elsewhere, the editorial accused the senior dean of the school of having a "sick mind." (*Id.* at 989)

Consequently minor plaintiff Scoville was removed as editor of the school newspaper and recommendations were sent to the school board that he be expelled from Joliet Central. Scoville and his father took action for declaratory and imaginative relief against the school district and officers on account of expulsion of high-school students for distribution of the student publication. They contended that "the expulsion order constituted a denial of the rights of the minor plaintiffs of free speech and free press; and that the expulsion order constituted an exercise of authority in excess of the power delegated to the school board by the State of Illinois." (*Id.* at 990)

A United States District Court upheld the school district in the suspension of Scoville, and supported its decision with the following comments:

> It is apparent from the face of the complaint here that the minor plaintiffs had engaged in speech on school grounds which amounted to an immediate advocacy of, and incitement to, disregard of school administrative procedures. Particularly in elementary and secondary schools, the state has a compelling interest in maintaining an atmosphere conducive to an orderly program of classroom learning, and to respect for legitimate and necessary administrative rules . . . where speech takes the form of immediate incitement to disregard of legitimate administrative regulations necessary to orderly maintenance of a public high school system; and where the speech occurs, not on a street or on a public park, where the rights of free speech are virtually absolute, but rather on the very property dedicated to a special public use, the education of younger citizens; and where the speech is directed to an audience which, because of its immaturity, is more likely than an adult audience to reach to the detriment of the school system, then it is the opinion of this Court that the interest

of the state in maintaining the school system out-
weighs the protection afforded the speaker by the
First Amendment. (*Id.* at 992)

Just one year after *Scoville*, the issue of high-school
students' freedom of speech and press was again
brought before a United States District Court for ad-
judication. This case (*Schwartz* v. *Schuker* (N.Y.),
298 F. Supp. 238, 1969) is quite similar to its prede-
cessor in that the court upheld the school board for expulsion of a high-school student (Jeffrey Schwartz) for
dissemination of a school publication containing derogatory statements regarding members of the school
administration.

The student involved claimed he was illegally suspended for "exercising his First Amendment right of
free speech" when he distributed copies of a newspaper
entitled "High School Free Press," off the school
grounds but near the high school. The newspaper criticized the principal of the school and other members of
the administration. For example, a previous issue of
the newspaper "contained four-letter words, filthy references, abusive and disgusting language and nihilistic
propaganda" and the immediate issue "criticized Principal Schuker, referring to him as 'King Louis, a big
liar,' and a person having 'racist views and attitudes.'"
(*Id.* at 240)

According to the school principal's affidavit, "both
parents asserted that their son had a right to carry on
student strikes and to attack the 'Establishment' at all
times and in any manner that Jeffrey deemed proper."
(*Id.* at 240)

After hearing various testimonies, the court pointed out that:

> the freedom of speech and association protected by the First and Fourteenth Amendments are not "absolute" and are subject to constitutional restrictions for the protection of the social interest in government, order and morality . . . the activities of high school students do not always fall within the same category as the conduct of college students, the former being in a much more adolescent and immature stage of life and less able to screen facts from propaganda. (*Id.* at 242)

In its concluding dicta the court declared:

> While there is a certain aura of sacredness attached to the First Amendment, nevertheless the First Amendment rights must be balanced against the duty and obligation of the state to educate students in an orderly and decent manner to protect the rights not of a few but of all the students in the school system. The line of reason must be drawn somewhere in this area of ever expanding permissibility. Gross disrespect and contempt for the officials of an educational institution may be justification not only for suspension but also expulsion of a student. (*Id.* at 242)

Somewhat akin to cases involving abusive language printed in student newspapers are those concerning the abusive language spoken directly. This was impressively illustrated in a United States District Court case (*Brown* v. *Greer* (Miss.), 296 F. Supp. 595, 1969) involving high school students who were suspended from school for "excessive verbal and physical attacks" upon school personnel.

According to the case report, five minor Negro children, through their parents (one of whom was referred to as "Big Mamma") brought a civil rights action against a school board for suspension of the five students "who used abusive and threatening language toward the superintendent and others, struck two faculty members, and disrupted the orderly operation of the school." (*Id.* at 595)

Testimony alleged that the offenses of the students against the school personnel were unusually violent. A reading of the complete case report which describes, at length, the tumultuous activity during the incident, confirms the allegation.

The court was convinced that:

> The actions of the school officials were not racially motivated, and in fact, the only mention of race made in this entire incident was that made by the plaintiff who stated that "Big Mamma was going to whip Mr. Gerrard's *white ass.*" The court finds that these plaintiffs are merely seeking to inject the issue of race in an effort to justify the unusual degree of commotion, boisterous conduct, collision with rights of others, defiance of authority and lack of order, discipline and decorum of which they were guilty on this day in question. Certainly, if the Court found that they were being discriminated against because of their race, color or creed, or that the actions of school officials were motivated thereby, it would, without hesitation, reach a contrary conclusion herein. (*Id.* at 601)

The court added: "This Court is concerned that if actions of the type involved herein by the plaintiffs are not punished and discouraged, they will not only lead to anarchy but will result in a suppression of the liberty and autonomy that are the lifeblood of a democracy and its educational institutions. . . ." (*Id.* at 602)

> In conclusion, the Court finds that there was an abundance of clear, convincing and unequivocal testimony which supports the action of the Board of Trustees in suspending the plaintiffs for the school year 1968-69. The Court also finds that the plaintiffs are not entitled to the equity relief which they seek because they have not come into equity with clean hands. (*Id.* at 602)

§ 4.5. Searching students' lockers.

The problem of suppressing the possession and use of harmful drugs by high school students constitutes a responsibility of school officials which is serious and potentially litiguous. One method used by school administrators to detect possession of the drugs is to search the students' lockers. The legality of such procedure, however, is sometimes challenged because of its conflict with the "searches and seizures" provision of the Fourth Amendment of the United States Constitution. An illustrative case (*In re Donaldson*, 75 Cal. Rptr. 220, 1969) arose in California when the vice principal of a high school searched a fifteen-year-old student's locker where he found cigarettes made of marijuana and a plastic bag containing marijuana.

A juvenile court found the accused student guilty of violating a section of the Health and Safety Code (possession of marijuana). On appeal it was contended that prejudicial error was committed by the court in admitting into evidence the cigarettes and plastic bag which had been obtained by an unlawful search and seizure carried out by a school official upon appellant's locker, since the school official was in fact a governmental official within the meaning of the Fourth Amendment. (*Id.* at 221)

The Court of Appeals, however, found

the vice principal of the high school not to be a governmental official within the meaning of the Fourth Amendment so as to bring into play its prohibition against unreasonable searches and seizures. Such school official is one of the school authorities with an obligation to maintain discipline in the interest of a proper and orderly school operation, and the primary purpose of the school official's search was not to obtain conviction, but to secure evidence of student misconduct. . . . The school officials, as a body and individually, have a responsibility for maintaining order upon the school premises so that the education, teaching and training of the students may be accomplished in an atmosphere of law and order. (*Id.* at 222)

The court concluded by declaring:

The school stands *in loco parentis* and shares, in matters of school discipline, the parent's right to use moderate force to obtain obedience, and that right extends to the search of the appellant's locker. . . . The marijuana was not obtained by an unlawful search and seizure. (*Id.* at 223)

Litigation regarding the search of students' lockers has also occurred where detectives or police have been given permission by school authorities to search the lockers where there was suspicion of illegal contents.

A case (*People* v. *Overton,* 20 N.Y.2d 360, 229 N.E.2d 596, 1967) in point arose in the Mount Vernon High School where detectives were permitted by the vice principal, Dr. Panitz, to search a student's locker in which they found marijuana cigarettes. Because of procedural irregularities a lower court held that the search was illegal. Upon appeal, however, the Court of Appeals of New York reversed the lower court decision and upheld the legality of the search despite admissible procedural deficiencies.

In its ruling the court placed emphasis on the distinct relationship between school authorities and students, as well as the concern of parents:

> The school authorities have an obligation to maintain discipline over the students. It is recognized that, when large numbers of teenagers are gathered together in such an environment, their inexperience and lack of mature judgment can often create hazards to each other. Parents, who surrender their children to this type of environment, in order that they may continue developing both intellectually and socially, have a right to expect certain safeguards. (*Id.* at 597)

The court concluded by saying:

> Indeed it is doubtful if a school would be properly discharging its duty of supervision over students, if it failed to retain control over the lockers. Not only have the school authorities a right to inspect but this right becomes a duty when suspicion arises that something of an illegal nature may be secreted there. When Dr. Panitz learned of the detective's suspicion, he was obligated to inspect the locker. This interest, together with the nonexclu-

sive nature of the locker, empowered him to consent to the search by the officers. (*Id.* at 598)

Cases emanating from the search of student lockers are not restricted to those in which harmful drugs are sought. Evidence may be sought in student lockers for other incriminating objects of wrongdoing. For example, in a Kansas case (*State* v. *Stein*, 203 Kan. 638, 456 P.2d 1, 1969), a high-school student's locker was searched for evidence of a crime for which he was suspected. The student, Madison Stein, had been charged with second degree burglary and grand larceny. He was convicted on both charges and appealed.

On the day following the burglary, "two police officers visited the high school principal who, at their request, and with Mr. Stein's consent and on his own judgment, opened Stein's school locker and brought its contents to his office." (*Id.* at 2)

Stein contended that the evidence found was inadmissible because he had not been given a *Miranda* warning to the search. This contention, among others, was rejected by the Kansas State Supreme Court, as it upheld the legality of the search.

The court's reasoning in the case confirmed that described in the *Overton* case. Moreover, it gave greater emphasis to the peculiar legal nature of a student's locker:

> Although a student may have control of his school locker as against fellow students, his possession is not exclusive against the school and its officials. A school does not supply its students with lockers for illicit use in harboring pilfered prop-

erty or harmful substances. We deem it a proper function of school authorities to inspect the lockers under their control and to prevent their use in illicit ways or for illegal purposes. We believe this right of inspection is inherent in the authority vested in school administration and that the same must be retained and exercised in the management of our schools if their educational functions are to be maintained and the welfare of the student bodies preserved. (*Id.* at 3)

§ 4.6. Controlling behavior away from and after school.

Home study. — Although the *in loco parentis* doctrine is generally accepted while the pupil is in school, there is less certainty as to its application off the campus and outside the regular school session. A precedential case (*Hobbs* v. *Germany*, 94 Miss. 469, 49 So. 515, 1909) is applicable and is often cited. The antiquity of the case and the circumstances which prompted it might suggest that it has no present-day relevance. However, the legal principle derived from it is as applicable today as it was at the time the case was adjudicated. It indicates the school's limitations in the control over pupils away from school and after school hours.

The case grew out of a school requirement that all pupils must stay in their homes and study from 7 to 9 p. m. One evening during the designated home-study period a sixteen-year-old boy was apprehended attending a religious service with his father, whereupon school authorities attempted to exact punishment by having the boy withdrawn from school for violation of the rule. Consequently the father filed suit, alleging that "the adoption of the rule is beyond the lawful power of either the trustees or the teachers, and constitutes a usurpation of authority not conferred upon them by law." (*Id.* at 516) Agreement of the Supreme Court of Mississippi is indicated by following excerpts extracted from the opinion: .

> Certainly a rule of the school, which invades the home and wrests from the parent his right to control his child around his own hearthstone, is inconsistent with any law that has governed the parent in this state, and the writer of this opinion dares hope that it will be inconsistent with any law that will ever operate here so long as liberty lasts, and children are taught to revere and look to their parents. In the home the parental authority is and should be supreme, and it is a misguided zeal that attempts to wrest it from them. . . . The directors are not authorized to prescribe a rule which undertakes to regulate the conduct of children within the district, who have a right to attend the school, after they are dismissed from it and remitted to the custody and care of the parent or guardian. They have the unquestioned right to make needful rules for the control of pupils while at school, and under the charge of the person or persons who teach it, and it would be the duty of the teacher to enforce such rules, when made. While in the teacher's charge, the parent would have no right to invade the schoolroom and interfere with him in its management. On the other hand, when the pupil is released, and sent back to its home, neither the teachers nor directors have the authority to follow him thither, and govern his conduct while under the parental age. (*Id.* at 517)

In the preceding case referred to it was noted that the court ruled that, under the circumstances, the school could not legally exercise control over the pupil away from and after school, but the court went on to say:

> It may be that the school authorities would have a right to make certain regulations and rules for the good government of the school, which would extend and control the child even when it had reached its home; but, if that power exists, it can only be done in matters which would per se have a direct and pernicious effect on the moral tone of the school, or have a tendency to subvert and destroy the proper administration of school affairs. . . . When such a case comes before the court, it will be time enough to decide how far the authority may be extended. (*Id.* at 517-18)

Misbehavior away from school. — Such cases did develop and were decided as predicted. For example, in a Connecticut case (*O'Rourke* v. *Walker*, 102 Conn. 130, 128 A. 25, 1925) an assault action was brought against a school principal who punished a boy for abusing small girl pupils on their way home from school. Even though the incident took place after the boy had reached home, the court sustained a judgment in favor of the principal, and said:

> Examination of the authorities clearly reveals the true test of the teacher's right and jurisdiction to punish for offenses not committed on the school property or going and returning therefrom, but after the return of the pupil to the parental abode, to be not the time or place of the offense, but its effect upon the morale and efficiency of the school, whether it in fact is detrimental to its good order, and to the welfare and advancement of the pupils therein. . . . (*Id.* at 26)

To the plaintiff's argument that "the proper resort to correct such an abuse is the parents of such offenders, or public prosecutors," the court replied:

> Some parents would dismiss the matter by saying that they could give no attention to children's quarrels; many would even champion their children as being all right in their conduct. The public authorities would very properly say, unless the offense resulted in quite serious injury, that such affrays were too trifling to deserve their attention. Yet the harm to the school has been done, and its proper conduct and operation seriously harmed, by such acts. Correction will usually be sought in vain at the hands of the parents; it can only be successfully applied by the teachers. (*Id.* at 27)

Authority during lunch period. — There has been some uncertainty as to the extent of control school personnel possess over pupils during the lunch period. An illustrative case (*Richardson* v. *Braham*, 125 Neb. 142, 249 N.W. 557, 1933) resulted from a school board resolution that:

> the senior high school be and is a one-session school with a lunch period of not more than 25 minutes, and that no students be permitted to leave the school grounds between 9 a. m. and 3:05 p. m., except such students as live quite close to the high school building, and whose parents request in writing that they be permitted to go home for lunch. (*Id.* at 558)

Certain parents who wished for their children to patronize a cafeteria adjacent to the school grounds sought an injunction to enjoin enforcement of the board's resolution. Two of the several complaints were that the regulation interfered "with prerogative of parents to prescribe diet and select food for their children" and enforced "patronage of high school cafeteria and boycotting Haffner cafeteria." (*Id.* at 558)

Although the district court rendered a decree enjoining the enforcement of the regulation, it was reversed by the Supreme Court of Nebraska, with the following comment:

> While there may be some diversity of judicial opinion on the subject, the better view seems to be that a board of education having power to make rules and regulations for the conduct and management of public schools may provide for one session daily and forbid pupils to leave the campus during school hours. (*Id.* at 559)

More recently another case (*Fitzpatrick v. Board of Education of Central School District No. 2*, 54 Misc. 2d 1085, 284 N.Y.S.2d 590, 1967), dealing with permission for pupils to leave school to eat lunch at home, was adjudicated in New York. Here the Board of Education passed a resolution prohibiting students from leaving the school grounds during the lunch recess, and resolved that the students had to have their luncheons in the school cafeteria. However, at the parents' request, permission was granted for students to eat their lunch at home — provided the father or mother would pick up the children at school and return them after the lunch period. After the parents failed to fulfill this condition, the students were suspended.

The parents of the students sought to have the suspension rescinded and annulled, alleging that "the

Board rules were arbitrary, capricious, and unreasonable, and therefore, unconstitutional and illegal." (*Id.*
at 591) Disregarding this allegation, the Court ruled
in favor of the school authorities and stated:

> The Board of Education has the authority and
> the duty to adopt rules and regulations for the
> orderly and efficient operation of the school. There
> is a presumption that these rules and regulations
> are reasonable and necessary. The Court should
> not interfere, even if it may disagree with a par-
> ticular rule or regulation, unless it is obviously
> capricious or arbitrary. (*Id.* at 592)

Destruction of school property. — Under the common law, until recently, the legal principle prevailed
that neither a minor child nor his parent is financially
responsible for the acts of a child. However, a New Jersey case (*Board of Education of Palmyra* v. *Hansen*,
56 N.J. 567, 153 A.2d 393, 1959) illustrates what may
be a trend that the parent should be held liable for the
damaging acts of his children, no matter whether committed during or after school hours.

In this case a court rendered a decision in favor of a
school board that sought to recover damages in the
amount of $344,000 from the parents of a boy who pur-
posely set fire to a school building. The board brought
the suit under the parent responsibility law in New
Jersey which stipulates:

> Any pupil who shall cut, deface, or otherwise in-
> jure any schoolhouse, furniture, fences, outbuild-
> ings, or other property of the school district shall
> be liable to suspension and punishment, and his
> parents or guardian shall be liable for damages to

the amount of the injury to be collected by the
board of education. ... (*Id.* at 395)

A defense of the counsel for the parents was that the
act was committed out of school hours and the presence
of a teacher. In answering the defense claim that the
statute applied only during school hours, the court
replied:

> ... if the Legislature has the right to confer bene-
> fits on people by way of a free education, it cer-
> tainly has the right to set up the conditions under
> which such benefits shall be provided. The Legisla-
> ture has authority to impose restrictions on those
> seeking to attend the public schools and can sus-
> pend or expel for events happening out of school
> hours. (*Id.* at 395)

The court added that "The parents do not have to
send their child to a public school and thereby be subject to conditions under which free public education is
provided." (*Id.* at 396) In conclusion the court stated:
". . . it is clear that with the parents of the defendant
pupil, there was a choice of electing to send their son to
a public school and accept the statutory imposed. By
such decision they made themselves amendable [*sic*] to
the liability of the statute." (*Id.* at 397)

§ 4.7. Restraining affiliation with secret societies.

Court cases dealing with the issue of secret societies
in the public schools bear a relationship to cases pertaining to the control of pupil behavior away from and
after school; after all, the objectionable activities of the
secret societies are usually carried on outside the school
and after school hours.

Secret societies have been considered so detrimental to high school morale as to cause at least 25 states to enact anti-fraternity laws. In most of the other 25 states school boards have adopted policies designed to curb the activities and existence of these organizations.

Students and parents have challenged, in courts, the authority of the legislature to enact anti-fraternity statutes, as well as the school board regulations to impose restrictions and penalties on those who affiliate with the secret societies. Either the state statutes or board regulations have been tested in the courts of record of 17 states in the past century. Reference to just a few of the cases will illustrate the contentions between parents and school officials regarding the issue, as well as the judicial reactions.

In a typical anti-fraternity case (*Holroyd* v. *Eibling*, 116 Ohio App. 440, 188 N.E.2d 797, 1962) an Ohio court was petitioned for a permanent injunction to enjoin the school board of Columbus from enforcing a regulation which prohibited any pupil holding membership in a fraternity or sorority from participating in "... any athletic, literary, military, musical, dramatic, service, scientific, scholastic, and other similar activities of his school including honor societies, or honor organizations...." (*Id.* at 799)

Plaintiff parents objected to the regulations on the grounds that if enforced, the school authorities would gain complete control of the pupils' activities and thus deny parents their responsibility to select associates for their children away from school and after school hours.

The court was not impressed by this argument, and accordingly upheld the action of the school board.

After reviewing and referring to a number of preceding court decisions on the issue, the Court of Appeals of Ohio stated:

> The rationale of these decisions is that a board of education is vested with broad discretionary powers in adopting a policy prohibiting affiliation with such organizations in the government, management and discipline of the schools; that such regulations do not deprive the pupils or parents of any *natural* or constitutional rights or privileges; that, when, in the opinion of the school authorities, such organizations have a deleterious influence and are found to be inimical to the best interests of the school, a school board is authorized, even in the absence of a specific statute granting such power, to adopt regulations prohibiting them; and that such power is inherent in a board of education. (*Id.* at 801)

In a Texas case (*Passel* v. *Fort Worth Independent School District* (Tex.), 429 S.W.2d 917, 1968) a class suit was instituted in which a number of parents sought to prevent enforcement of a statute prohibiting secret societies in the public schools, and a school board rule which required the parents of all students entering junior and senior high schools to sign a Supplementary Application Enrollment Form "certifying that the student was not a member and that he or she would not become a member of a high-school fraternity, sorority or secret society." Certification by the parent was merely an addendum to the applicable provision of the

Texas Penal Code prohibiting membership in secret societies of the public schools.

The Court of Civil Appeals of Texas did not express much concern about several grievances of the plaintiff parents, with the exception of the one claiming that the school board requirement was an invasion of the right of parents to control their children. The court expressed its disagreement with this contention in the following terms:

> The argument advanced by the appellants which causes us the most concern is that the statute involved constitutes an invasion of the right of parental control over their children. Certainly neither the school system or the church or any other organization however well motivated should or could replace parents in the rearing of a child. We would not wish to say anything in this opinion which would weaken this basic and fundamental right. But we do not believe that requiring parents to sign the Supplemental Enrollment Form constitutes an invasion of parental control as to render it constitutionally invalid. We believe that our duly constituted independent school districts with appropriate guidance from the Legislature should run our public school system. While the last thing we would wish to do is to interfere with the right of freedom of association or the civil rights of the students involved, we must maintain an orderly system of administration of our public schools. (*Id.* at 925)

Litigation involving the legality of secret societies in the public schools is not limited to fraternities. A case (*Robinson* v. *Sacramento City Unified School Dis-*

trict, 245 Cal. App. 278, 53 Cal. Rptr. 781, 1966) arose in California, where a member of a girls' club, called the "Manana Club," sought (through her father, as guardian ad litem) to have a rule of the school board declared invalid which prohibited a fraternity, sorority, or club in which the membership was determined secretly. The school board adopted the rule in accordance with a provision of the Education Code which "makes it unlawful for any pupil, enrolled in any elementary or secondary school of this State to join any secret fraternity, sorority, or club wholly or partly formed by membership of pupils attending the public schools."

The plaintiffs contended that the Manana Club was not secret, even though candidates were selected by an admission committee of 16 girls in a process so secret that the general membership was never apprised of those who comprise its [the committee's] membership. On this basis, the court concluded that the evidence was sufficient to justify the characterization of the club as "secret" as a matter of law.

Although the court admittedly saw some merits in a secret society, such as those alleged by the club involved, it left it to the judgment of the school board to determine if they were sufficient enough to justify its existence. The court declared:

> High school fraternities, sororities and clubs undoubtedly accomplish good, mostly to those who belong to them, giving them a sense of security, a feeling of being wanted. But the school board has said the harm these societies do outweighs the

good, that they are inimical to the government, discipline and morale of the pupils. School boards are professionals in this field, the courts are laymen; the boards are close to the day-to-day affairs of the pupils of secondary schools and the problems which arise in a school community, courts are removed therefrom. (*Id.* at 789)

In holding the school board rule valid, the court concluded thusly:

Here the school board is not dealing with adults but with adolescents in their formative years. And it is not dealing with activities which occur only within the home and which, therefore, might be said to relate exclusively to parental jurisdiction and control. It is dealing with express statutory mandate with activities which reach into the school and which reasonably may be said to interfere with the educational process, with the morale of high-school student bodies as a whole and which also may reasonably be said not to foster democracy (as the Manana Club by its admitted activities practices). (*Id.* at 790)

Chapter 5

CONCLUSIONS AND IMPLICATIONS

GENERALLY

§ 5.1. Scope of chapter.

Court cases referred to in the preceding chapters dealt with (1) compulsory and prohibitory school attendance, (2) authority of curricular activities, and (3) control over student behavior. The cases reported were those which were most germane to the purpose of the investigation. An attempt was made to report those cases which dealt specifically with parental versus state authority over the pupil. Virtually all the cases selected were those decided by courts of record (federal and higher state courts). Although some of the earlier precedential cases were treated, major emphasis was placed upon the most recent ones. In contrast to the objective treatment of cases in the preceding chapters, the procedure to be followed in this concluding chapter is to present personal judgments with respect to trends and implications of the selected court decisions involving allocation of authority over the pupil.

COMPULSORY AND PROHIBITORY SCHOOL ATTENDANCE

§ 5.2. Generally.

The first court cases, involving the allocation of authority to determine the extent of schooling of children, indicate that the public concept was that the parents should be granted complete discretionary control over the education and nurture of their offspring. Gradually, however, the public, and especially the judiciary, recognized the injustice of the early common law which authorized absolute parental control over the child's education, which could potentially result in the deprivation of the child's welfare as well as that of society. Consequently compulsory school attendance laws were passed. In the early stages the constitutionality of these laws was challenged on the grounds that they violated the natural rights of parents to control the welfare of their children. Despite some judicial vacillation over the issue, the legal precedent was finally, firmly — and likely — permanently established, through court decisions, that the state *has* sufficient power to enact compulsory school attendance legislation.

§ 5.3. Alternatives to public school attendance.

Even after the concept of compulsory school attendance had been generally accepted, parents frequently attempted to comply with the requirement by having their children attend a school other than a *public* school. State laws which were designed to do away with parochial schools by requiring attendance at public schools only were vigorously challenged in the courts. Such laws were declared unconstitutional by the United States Supreme Court as early as 1925, and since that time, attendance at nonpublic schools, which meets the required educational standards, fulfills state compulsory school attendance requirements.

In many other instances parents have sought compliance with compulsory school attendance requirements by having their children taught at home. Whether home instruction, in lieu of public or nonpublic school instruction, is accepted by the courts as fulfilling requirements, depends, in large part, on the phrasing of the applicable statutes. Leading court cases indicate that home instruction will have judicial sanction as an alternative for school instruction, providing the home instruction is equivalent to that which would be obtainable in a public school, and if there are no statutory provisions to the contrary. In some instances, however, the courts have held that home instruction *cannot* be equivalent to that of public school instruction in *social* development of the child.

Many of the court cases, where parents have insisted on home instruction rather than public school instruction, are prompted by religious motives. Parents of certain religious faiths frequently allege that the compulsory school attendance laws are contrary to the First and Fourteenth Amendments of the United States Constitution. The courts are emphatic in declaring such allegations invalid.

Obviously, under certain conditions of physical or mental deficiencies, it would be unwise and unjust to compel children to attend a regular school against the parents' wishes. Even though attendance officers and school officials may not always take such factors into consideration, the courts do. For the benefit of handicapped children, most states provide for "special schools." Sometimes, however, parents refuse to enter their children into "special schools," alleging their children would be victims of ridicule by children attending the regular schools. The courts do not accept such a reason as justification to keep a child from attending the special school.

§ 5.4. Vaccination as a condition for attendance.

Cases have arisen where children have been denied admission to the public schools for failure to comply with vaccination requirements. Then the courts may be confronted with the question if such exclusion exempts the children from compliance with the attendance requirement. At first the courts tended to apply a strict construction to the attendance law, holding that if the parents had sent their children to school but were denied admission because of noncompliance with other valid regulations, the parents had fulfilled requirements of the compulsory school attendance law. The more modern judicial viewpoint, however, is that a parent would be held guilty of violating both requirements because it could not be an intent of the legislature that one law could be used as an excuse to disobey another.

Objections of parents to comply with vaccination requirements as a condition for school attendance are usually based on religious beliefs. The great majority of legislatures, as well as judiciaries, do not accept religious beliefs as a justifiable reason for refusal to have their children vaccinated. There are, however, rare instances in which a statute may express exemption to the vaccination requirement for children of school age if parents are members of a recognized religious organization whose teachings are contrary to vaccination practices. Only one such case was found in this investigation in which the exemption was sanctioned by a state supreme court. One could reasonably speculate that if this case had been appealed to the

United States Supreme Court, the decision of the state court might have been reversed in conformance to the well-established legal principle that "the freedom to believe as one chooses in the matter of religion is absolute, but the freedom to act in the exercise of religion is subject to regulation in the public interest and for the good order of society."

§ 5.5. Desegregation and compulsory attendance.

Very few of the numerous court cases involving desegregation of the races in the public schools refer directly to the compulsory school attendance laws. Nevertheless the potential legal question exists whether a parent's refusal to send his child to an assigned school which is "inferior," constitutes a violation of the compulsory school attendance requirements. On the basis of one court's ruling on this issue it appears that, if a Negro pupil is assigned to a school which is inferior to the other white schools, a parent will not be guilty of violating the compulsory school attendance law by refusing to send his child to the inferior Negro school.

§ 5.6. Dual enrolment and compulsory school attendance.

The specific question on the legality of dual enrolment (shared-time), whereby a pupil attends a public school part of the day and a nonpublic school the remainder of the day, has not been litigated very frequently. Only a couple of cases have been reported where the question of compliance with compulsory school attendance laws has been a dominant factor. The decisions of those cases indicate that the practice of shared-time programs is legal providing it does not result in substantial expenditure of public funds for nonpublic schools. As far as compulsory school attendance laws are involved in the dual enrolment cases reviewed, the courts are of the opinion that they are constitutional, since the object of the attendance law is that all children be educated but not necessarily in any particular manner or place.

§ 5.7. Attendance status of married girls and unwed mothers.

Marriages of school-age girls have prompted school boards to formulate policies, some of which are designed to *compel* attendance while others are for the purpose to *prohibit* school attendance. As far as the legality to *compel* school attendance is concerned, the issue was apparently settled convincingly in decisions of two cases in 1946 and 1949; at least similar cases have not been reported since then. The judicial ruling in that marriage *emancipates* a minor female and accordingly releases her from compulsory school attendance requirements. The issue regarding board policies to *prohibit* attendance of married girls is not so permanently settled, as is evidenced by the fact that applicable cases are being adjudicated continuously. On the basis of decisions rendered on the issue, the main legal principles derived therefrom are that (1) a school board *may not* legally prohibit attendance of married girls on a permanent basis; (2) a school board *may* legally prohibit attendance of a married girl for a limited time immediately following marriage; and (3) a school board *may* legally suspend a married girl from school during period of pregnancy.

A more recent factor entering the issue of board policies designed to regulate school attendance of school-age mothers concerns the *unwed mother*. The only ruling of a court on the issue reported to date is that unwed mothers cannot be excluded from school attendance merely because of the unwed status, unless they are found to be so lacking in moral character that their presence in the schools would taint the education of other students. Of course, that exception would likely apply also to married mothers, childless married students, and all other students regardless of marital status. The judicial view is that an unwed mother should have the opportunity for rehabilitation and to continue an education for the welfare of the individual as well as society.

AUTHORITY OVER CURRICULAR ACTIVITIES

§ 5.8. Generally.

Authority over the curriculum resides mostly with state officials and agencies. Only in rare instances do state constitutions stipulate curricular requirements. Frequently school patrons challenge the constitutionality of the curricular requirements instituted by state authorities and local school boards. Then the courts are called upon to settle the issues. When the litigated matters are related to provisions of the Federal Constitution, the federal courts may make the final decisions.

§ 5.9. Prescribing school subjects.

A review of all court cases dealing with curricular prescriptions reveals that there is a gradual decline in litigation on the issue. This is likely due to the fact that the legal principles on the subject are now rather firmly established. Moreover, with the increasing size of high schools more curricula are provided with more electives in each curriculum.

The earliest cases concerning prescriptions of subjects dealt mainly with the allocation of authority between school officials and parents in determining what the pupils should study. At first the courts applied, to considerable extent, the common law principle whereby parents held supreme authority during the minority of their children. More recently the courts have upheld state authorities in determining curricular content unless in conflict with state or federal constitutional provisions.

Although the question of including *sex education* in the curriculum is being hotly debated, actual litigation on the issue has not yet been very apparent. It is likely, however, that applicable court cases will be forthcoming.

§ 5.10. Theory of evolution.

The legality of statutes which prohibit the teaching of evolution has been tested in the courts for approximately a half century. At first the courts upheld the constitutionality of the statutes, as attested by the famous *Scopes* case of 1927. However, the United States Supreme Court finally — and perhaps conclusively — ruled in 1968 that anti-evolution laws are violative of the Fourteenth Amendment. Only one state retains an anti-evolution law in its statute books, and in all probability it would be declared unconstitutional if challenged in the federal courts.

§ 5.11. Flag salute.

Other mandated curricular activities have been challenged on the grounds of unconstitutionality. For example, the flag salute cases have reached the highest court in the land on, at least, two occasions. As with other required inclusions in the curriculum, there was considerable judicial vacillation before the United States Supreme Court finally ruled, in the *Barnette* case of 1943, that pupils could not legally be required to salute the flag. Despite the Supreme Court ruling, some school officials continue to press the requirement. For example, as late as 1966, pupils in a New Jersey school were suspended for refusal to salute the flag of the United States. As might have been anticipated, the State Supreme Court declared the requirement unconstitutional and accordingly ordered the reinstatement of the children into the school.

§ 5.12. Religious exercises.

A majority of court cases, in which pupil participation in curricular activities is an issue, have religious undertones. Consequently many of the cases are ultimately carried to federal courts to determine whether amendments to the federal constitution are violated.

Reading of the Bible in the public schools has been the subject of litigation time and again in the various states over the past century. State courts were not consistent in ruling on the legality of the practice. Finally, however, the United States Supreme Court ruled in the widely-publicized *Schempp* case (1963) that statutes requiring that verses from the Bible shall be read at morning exercises are unconstitutional. Although there is much evidence that Bible reading in the public schools still persists, in accordance with policies of local school officials, the federal courts have not been called upon to rule upon the practice if statutory requirements are not involved.

Recitation of prayers in the public schools has been ruled by the Supreme Court much in the same manner as has the practice of reading verses from the Bible. The high court, in *Engle-Vitale* (1962) ruled that a brief state-mandated prayer was inconsistent with the Establishment Clause of the First Amendment, and therefore unconstitutional. There were those who contended that the ruling applied only to *state-mandated* prayers and would not affect other prayers instituted by teachers. Nevertheless, in 1968, a federal court invalidated a brief verse (prayer) composed and used by a teacher for her kindergarten children.

It is doubtful that the controversial issue regarding the legality and propriety of reading verses from the Bible and reciting prayers in the public schools has been conclusively resolved. The public appears to be quite evenly divided as to the correctness of the Supreme Court decisions. Some believe the decisions were based upon a strict construction of the Constitution, and that the Court had no alternative in its rulings;

whereas others contend that the Court misinterpreted the real meaning of the Constitution, and that appropriate steps should be taken to "bring God back into the classroom." Several different methods are advocated. One method would be to disregard the decisions of the Supreme Court and to continue the religious exercises; that, of course, would be improper and illegal. Another method advocated by some prominent statesmen, would be to amend the United States Constitution so as to legalize the practices; that would be the democratic way, but not likely to succeed. The prospect of altering the Court's position is rather dim, at least for the immediate future; in each of the two Supreme Court's rulings there was only one dissenting opinion, and it would perhaps be a long time before a majority of different-minded judges would be appointed to the Court.

§ 5.13. Barring married students from non-classroom activities.

At least six cases pertaining to the exclusion of married students from non-classroom (extracurricular) activities have been tried in state supreme courts. Although, in every case, the court has upheld the school board's exclusion policies, the legal principles derived from the decisions do not appear to be stable. The fact that courts have so far upheld the *legality* of board regulations prohibiting married students from participating in extracurricular activities should not be construed as judicial concurrence on the *propriety* of the regulations. When courts repeat that they do not rule upon the "wisdom" or "unwisdom" of board regulations, one wonders if the court has reservations regarding the propriety of the rules.

On the basis of all the case reports on the issue it may be speculated that the time is coming when the courts will declare regulations barring married students from extracurricular activities as "unreasonable" and therefore "illegal." If school officials contend that the so-called "extracurricular activities" need not be made available to all students because they do not constitute part of the actual school curriculum, it is conceivable that someone might challenge the legality of an "extracurricular activity" that is directed by public school personnel, conducted on public school property, and paid for out of public school funds.

Of course school board rules will have judicial sanction in prohibiting students from school attendance or barring them from participation in certain school activities, when it is evident that their attendance or participation is injurious to the morale and conduct of the school. It should be emphasized, however, that *this applies to all students regardless of marital status.*

CONTROL OVER STUDENT BEHAVIOR

§ 5.14. Generally.

The majority of court cases related to authority over the pupil deal with behavior (discipline). This is particularly true for cases reported during the past decade and those which apply to students at the secondary level. Since a report of all cases dealing with legal aspects of student behavior is beyond the intended scope of this investigation, only a sampling of cases has been selected for review, with emphasis on those pertaining to alleged disruptive behavior where "freedom of expression" and "due process" provisions of the First and Fourteenth Amendments to the Constitution are involved.

§ 5.15. Regulating student appearance.

Judging from the numerous articles and court cases pertaining to hairstyles of boys it would appear that the regulation of hairstyles is one of the foremost functions to be performed by school officials in the control of student behavior. Even though the articles in periodicals and reports of court cases may provide reading which appears to be entertaining but insignificant, the legal ramifications of hairstyle cases *are significant*. In virtually all the cases the perennial question of invasion of family authority over the student is raised. Also each case reported thus far is centered around the issue as to whether the length or appearance of the hair is so disruptive as to interfere with the successful operation of the school.

With respect to the question of a school regulation constituting an invasion of family authority, the courts are generally agreed that the domain of family privacy "must give way in so far as a regulation reasonably calculated to maintain school discipline may affect it." The perplexing issue for the courts to resolve, however, is when is a board rule regulating manner of dress or hairstyle "reasonably calculated." Generally a regulation to control manner of dress or style of hair is considered to be reasonable when it is necessary to abate disruption in the classroom. Significantly though a particular hairstyle which may have been disruptive in a classroom several years ago may no longer be so regarded. The courts are cognizant of this as is indicated by the trend in court decisions regarding hairstyles of boys. Some years ago the wearing of long hair by one boy in a classroom would have been judged to be disruptive; whereas, today, the length of a boy's hair would have to be extreme indeed to cause disruption or even attention.

§ 5.16. Display of insignia as a protest.

The wearing of insignia such as armbands or buttons has been cause for litigation during a period of student protest and militancy. As was true in the "hairstyle cases," the courts have generally ruled that the wearing of insignia by high school students is legal if done so in a manner not disruptive to classroom discipline and decorum. The federal courts hold that the display of armbands and buttons constitutes "symbolic expression" which is a right guaranteed to students and others by virtue of the Free Speech Clause of the First Amendment. The undue concern of some school officials in the federal court rulings appears to be unwarranted. After all, the courts have not applied "freedom of speech" provisions where disruptive affects of wearing the insignia are proved. Moreover, school officials may not be compelled to act or refrain from acting in any particular way merely because the "symbolic expression" of students has judicial sanction.

§ 5.17. Students' restricted freedom of speech and press.

The publication and dissemination of articles and editorials in student newspapers is more specifically related to the "freedom of speech" clause of the Constitution than is the "symbolic expression" of wearing insignia. Nevertheless in the cases adjudicated thus far, the federal courts have not allowed students as much latitude in "written expression" — particularly when the written material is of a derogatory nature, and which could be injurious to the morale of the school. The courts differentiate between college students and high-school students in the degree of freedom allowed for expressing themselves. The more matured students are less likely to be swayed by propaganda.

§ 5.18. Searching students' lockers.

School officials are concerned about the presence of harmful drugs and other incriminating objects in school buildings which would be injurious to the welfare of the student body and the school. Evidence of possession is sought where it is most likely to be concealed — in the students' lockers. In searching the lockers, however, the school officials assume the risk of violating the "searches and seizures" provision of the Fourth Amendment to the United States Constitution. Some legal experts, including judges, manifest reservation as to the legality of searching the lockers. Nevertheless court decisions on the few cases that have been adjudicated indicate that school officials do have, not only the right, but also the obligation to take such measures as are necessary, such as searching lockers, to determine the presence of anything that could endanger the welfare of the school. This contention has been given confirmation by the last court case reported at the time of this writing, in which the court held that what is referred to as a "student locker" is, in fact, a "school locker." That legal principle convincingly empowers school authorities to inspect lockers under their control in order to prevent their use in illicit ways for illegal purposes.

§ 5.19. Controlling behavior away from and after school.

It is generally agreed that the education of children is no longer confined to the four walls of a classroom or to only the hours between 8 a.m. and 4 p.m. Consequently school authorities possess the right and duty to supervise *school-sponsored* activities regardless of where and when they occur. By virtue of the *in loco parentis* doctrine, school personnel are authorized to govern behavior of students on field trips or at athletic events if they are part of the school program. However, there is less certainty as to school authority over student behavior where the student is merely on the way to and from school and while he is not engaged in a school-sponsored activity. Since so many diverse factors would have to be taken into consideration, there is no legal principle applicable to the issue which could serve as a guideline for all cases. Some courts, however, suggest that disciplinary action might be legally applied by school personnel when the infractions of students "have a direct and pernicious effect on the moral tone of the school, or have a tendency to subvert and

destroy the proper administration of school affairs."
It may be concluded that the nature of the act, rather
than its place or time, determines the legality and propriety of the punishment to be inflicted by school personnel.

§ 5.20.   Restraining affiliation with secret societies.

Approximately a dozen cases dealing with secret
societies at the high school have been tried in courts
of record. In all instances they involved fraternities,
with the exception of one case which concerned a girls'
club in which membership was determined secretly.
Since most of the antifraternity cases were strikingly
similar, reference was made in Chapter 4 to only two
of the typical cases — one, where the exclusion of
extracurricular activities was used as a deterrent, and
the other where suspension was applied.

The usual technique of school authorities in suppressing the fraternities is to curtail or prohibit participation in extracurricular activities for those who
are affilated with the secret organizations. A more direct, but less-used, method is by suspension or expulsion. Regardless of the nature of the punitive measures imposed upon students because of affiliation with
the secret societies, parents have objected to the regulations on the grounds that they constitute an invasion
on the rights of parents to control their children and
to select their associates away from school and after
school hours.

Without exception, the courts have upheld antifraternity rules as being applicable during the regular

school term. (There is some judicial reservation as to their applicability during the summer period when the school is not in session.) The courts do not agree with the allegations that the antifraternity regulations deprive pupils or parents of any natural or constitutional rights.

On the basis of experience in school systems where fraternities were active, this writer is of the opinion that suspension is more legal and expeditious than deprivation of participation in extracurricular activities. It is true that suspension or expulsion is undesirable. Nevertheless such direct action does put the responsibility on the parents. Most parents would be less concerned about having their children barred from extracurricular activities than to be banished from the school and all its activities.

Table of Cases

De Spain v. De Kalb Community School District (Ill.), 384 F.2d 836 (1968), p. 66.

Dobbins v. Commonwealth, 198 Va. 697, 96 S.E.2d 154 (1957), p. 33.

In re Donaldson, 75 Cal. Rptr. 220 (1969), p. 108.

Doremus v. Board of Education, 5 N.J. 435, 75 A.2d 880 (1950), p. 61.

Doremus v. Board of Education, 342 U.S. 429 (1952), p. 63.

Edwards v. South Carolina, 372 U.S. 229 (1963), p. 100.

Engle v. Vitale, 370 U.S. 421 (1962), p. 64.

Epperson v. State of Arkansas, 89 S. Ct. 266 (1968), p. 56.

Ferrell v. Dallas Independent School District (Tex.), 261 F. Supp. 545 (1966), p. 78.

Finot v. Pasadena City Board of Education, 58 Cal. Rptr. 520 (1967), p. 88.

Fitzpatrick v. Board of Education of Central School District No. 2, 54 Misc. 2d 1085, 284 N.Y.S.2d 590 (1967), p. 116.

In re Gault, 387 U.S. 1 (1967), p. 5.

Griffin v. Tatum (Ala.), 300 F. Supp. 60 (1969), p. 82.

Guzick v. Drebus (Ohio), 305 F. Supp. 472 (1969), p. 98.

Hardwick v. Board of Trustees, 54 Cal. App. 696, 205 P. 49 (1921), p. 50.

Hobbs v. Germany, 94 Miss. 469, 49 So. 515 (1909), p. 112.

Holden v. Board of Education of the City of Elizabeth, 46 N.J. 281, 216 A.2d 387 (1966), p. 60.

Holroyd v. Eibling, 116 Ohio App. 440, 188 N.E.2d 797 (1962), p. 119.

Kelley v. Ferguson, 95 Neb. 63, 144 N.W. 1039 (1914), p. 48.

Kissick v. Garland Independent School District (Tex.), 330 S.W.2d 708 (1959), p. 68.

Leonard v. School Committee of Attleboro, 349 Mass. 704, 212 N.E.2d 468 (1965), p. 76.

McCartney v. Austin, 57 Misc. 2d 525, 293 N.Y.S.2d 188 (1968), p. 31.

McLeod v. State, 154 Miss. 468, 122 So. 737 (1929), p. 41.

Scott v. Board of Education, Union Free School District No. 17, Hicksville, 305 N.Y.S.2d 601 (1969), p. 89.

Scoville v. Board of Education of Joliet Township High School District 204 (Ill.), 286 F. Supp. 988 (1968), p. 103.

In re Shinn, 195 Cal. App. 2d 683, 16 Cal. Rptr. 165 (1961), p. 25.

Special District for the Education and Training of Handicapped Children v. Wheeler (Mo.), 408 S.W.2d 60 (1966), p. 38.

Starkey v. Board of Education, 14 Utah 2d 227, 381 P.2d 718 (1963), p. 70.

State v. Bailey, 157 Ind. 324, 61N.E. 730 (1901), p. 10.

State v. Garber (Kan.), 419 P.2d 896 (1966), p. 15.

State v. Ghrist, 222 Iowa 1069, 270 N.W. 376 (1936), p. 23.

In re State in Interest of Goodwin, 214 La. 1062, 39 So. 2d 731 (1949), p. 40.

State v. Jackson 71 N.H. 552, 53 A. 1021 (1902), p. 22.

State v. Massa, 95 N.J. Super. 382, 231 A.2d 252 (1967), p. 18.

State v. Miday, 263 N.C. 747, 140 S.E.2d 325 (1965), p. 31.

State v. Priest, 210 La. 389, 27 So.2d 173 (1946), p. 39.

State v. Stein, 203 Kan. 638, 456 P.2d 1 (1969), p. 111.

State v. Stevenson, 27 Ohio Op. 2d 223, 189 N.E.2d 181 (1962), p. 70.

Stephens v. Bongart, 15 N.J. Misc. 80, 189 A. 131 (1937), p. 20.

TASTE, Inc. v. Topeka Board of Education, Action No. 112064 (1969), p. 52.

Tinker v. Des Moines Independent School District (Iowa), 89 S. Ct. 733 (1969), p. 93.

Trustees of Schools v. People, 87 Ill. 303 (1877), p. 8.

Villarreal v. State (Tex.) 429 S.W.2d 659 (1968), p. 26.

West Virginia State Board of Education v. Barnette, 319 U.S. 624 (1943), p. 58.

Wright v. State, 21 Okla. 430, 209 P. 179 (1922), p. 17.

Index

(References are to Page Numbers)